Anonymous

The destiny of Russia, as foretold by God's prophets

Anonymous

The destiny of Russia, as foretold by God's prophets

ISBN/EAN: 9783337102944

Printed in Europe, USA, Canada, Australia, Japan

Cover: Foto ©Lupo / pixelio.de

More available books at **www.hansebooks.com**

SHOWING THE FU[T

THE
DESTINY OF RUSSIA,

AS FORETOLD BY GOD'S PROPHETS,

TOGETHER WITH AN OUTLINE OF THE FUTURE MOVEMENTS AND DESTINY OF

ENGLAND, GERMANY, PERSIA, AFRICA,

AND THE JEWS.

BY THETA.

CHICAGO:
THOMAS WILSON, 188 East Monroe Street,
1878.

MAP OF EUROPE AND ASIA
SHOWING THE FUTURE MOVEMENTS OF RUSSIA & ENGLAND WITH THEIR ALLIES & DEPENDENCIES
AS FORETOLD BY THE PROPHETS OF GOD.

PREFACE.

In undertaking the task of setting forth the Destiny of Russia, and other existing powers, we avow our utter inability to shed a ray of certain light upon so important a subject, unless it had first been revealed from heaven. He who knoweth the end from the beginning has graciously made known in His holy word, events yet future; or in other words, He has, by His Prophets, written beforehand the history of Russia, England, and other powers, so far, at least, as they stand related to His ancient people Israel.

Seeing that the whole world was being stirred by reason of the war between Russia and Turkey, and hearing so many opinions expressed as to the final outcome, we felt impelled to present in a brief way, God's testimony upon the subject. That this testimony will be received by all, we do not expect. As we draw nearer to the end of the Gentile age, we find the community of Infidels being largely augmented. From these we expect nothing but ridicule. God, with them, is but a myth, hence any communication purporting to come from Him can have no weight. But there is another class whose faith takes hold of God as Abraham's did. These will neither reject nor scoff at the testimony of God, but will receive it gladly, especially seeing that it tells of a glorious reign of righteousness and peace, just beyond the troubled sea that is even now beginning to strike terror into the hearts of millions.

In preparing our little work, we acknowledge with gratitude, the help we have received from such writers as J. A. Begg, Dr. Seiss, Mr Trotter, and others, from whose works we have occasionally made liberal extracts.

If a single soul shall be separated from the world, and drawn to Christ the Savior, as a result of our feeble efforts to present God's truth concerning the near future, we shall be more than repaid for all our labor. That the Lord may bless the work so as to redound in some measure to His own glory, is the humble prayer of

THE AUTHOR.

EXPLANATION OF MAP.

Yellow indicates the present and future possessions of Russia, together with those of her allies at the time of the confederacy.

Pink indicates the same for England, Russia's great opponent.

The Bible names are introduced, showing the original location of Magog, Meshech, Tubal, Gomer, Togarmah, etc., in Asia Minor, not far from the Caucasian Mountains, together with the direction of their spreading to the North, North-east and North-west.

CONTENTS.

CHAPTER I.
THE IMPORTANCE OF PROPHETIC STUDY.

Consequences of its neglect — The dream of unwatchful virgins — The Millennium, and how it will be ushered in — The abundance of Prophecy — Objections to its study answered — Its literal fulfilment 20

CHAPTER II.
THE ISRAELITES, AS RELATED TO PROPHECY IN THE PAST.

The destiny of all nations interwoven with that of Israel — Israel's history foretold by Moses — The Seventy Years captivity — Their return and subsequent punishment by Antiochus Epiphanes — Overthrow and destruction of Jerusalem — A brief History of the persecution of the Jews from A. D. 70 to modern times — Their identity and worship still preserved — Our indebtedness to them — Signs of great changes 36

CHAPTER III.
THE ISRAELITES AS RELATED TO PROPHECY IN THE FUTURE.

Israel to be converted — Testimony as to their future regathering to the Holy Land — Their wonderful preservation — Signs of the Times — Judgments to precede — Results of their final re-settlement 56

CHAPTER IV.
THE EASTERN QUESTION.

Changes already in progress — What the Eastern Question is — Turkey doomed — Russia's ancient and settled policy — Napoleon

Bonaparte's prophecy — The declaration of Alexander II — The famous Will of Peter the Great — The time to favor Zion near — Final settlement of the Eastern Question in Palestine . . 67

CHAPTER V.
AN UNFULFILLED PROPHECY OF EZEKIEL.

A translation of Ezekiel xxxviii. and xxxix. by Isaac Leeser, an Israelite, accompanied with variable readings from the Douay and Septuagint versions 74

CHAPTER VI.
IDENTIFICATION OF THE POWERS.

Modern Powers with ancient names — The great confederacy — Criticism on "the chief prince," — Identification of Gog and Magog — of Rosh, Meshech and Tubal — of Persia and Ethiopia — of Libya, Gomer and Togarmah — of Sheba, Dedan, the Merchants of Tarshish and the Young Lions thereof — Summary . . 92

CHAPTER VII.
THE PROPHECY EXPLAINED.

The Emperor of Russia the great leader — The hook of six teeth — Fulfilment still future — Significance of recent events, and what we may expect — Absorption of petty states — Germany and other allies of Russia — Their intent and how met by England — Fearful judgments from God — The allied armies completely destroyed — Effect of the news — Christ's coming and the speedy deliverance of Israel 108

CHAPTER VIII.
CONCLUSION.

The hope of Israel realized — The final destiny of Russia, Germany, England and all other nations — The "Lord's prayer" answered — Christ's coming near — A warning to the unconverted — A parting word to those in Christ — Appendix . . . 118

THE DESTINY OF RUSSIA.

CHAPTER I.

THE IMPORTANCE OF PROPHETIC STUDY.

Inasmuch as the evidence we shall adduce for our conclusions respecting the future movements of Russia, and other powers, is based upon the prophecies of the Bible, and knowing, as we do, that there is a wide-spreading skepticism in the world relative to the importance of prophetic study we deem it proper at the outset to say a few words upon this subject.

Prophecy itself is, in part, God's testimony to the world—a testimony indeed of warning and of terror, fitly represented by Ezekiel's roll, written within and on the outside, and full of mourning, lamentation, and woe. And, in fact, one of the saddest consequences of the general neglect of the prophetic word has been that, instead of bearing in the world's ears continually this solemn and mournful testimony as to the world's course and end, the church has chimed in with Satan's lullaby of "Peace, peace," by which he soothes this poor guilty world into deeper slumber; while God's judgments, alas! by which it is even now being overtaken, slumber not. The world dreams of a golden age, a period of peace and plenty—of liberty and good government, drawing nigh; and it labors, as it has done for so many ages, to hasten its arrival. The unwatchful virgins, too, have slept or slumbered, instead of waking the live-long night to meet the Bridegroom at his coming; and they, too, have had their dreams, and have fancied the gradual and peaceful approach of the same blissful period. And while the world has sought to expedite its arrival by all the means and appliances of philosophy and science, and political economy, and a philanthropy having these for its foundation, how many professors of christianity have added to these the Gospel, and have thought thus to perfect the machinery by which this guilty, miserable world is to be brought back to universal purity and joy. Yes, and if it should be urged, as it doubtless would by some, that Christianity should be placed in the forefront, and all other things be only considered as subsidiary forces in the contest, what have you gained? The world and the church are still joined in one common phalanx, to fight one common battle, animated by one common hope of victory, and ensuring rest and peace and contentment in this world below. All join in putting far off the evil day, or in denying that there is such a day approaching.

Are we denying, then, that there is a day of universal peace and blessedness yet to dawn upon this oppressed and groaning earth? God forbid! There is a millennium yet to come; a period of universal righteousness and joy, brighter than any that man's hopes have pictured—brighter than any that even Christians have anticipated; a period in which men shall, indeed, "beat their swords into plowshares, and their spears into pruning hooks;" in which "nation shall not lift up sword against nation, neither shall they learn war any more;" but when "the glory of the Lord shall be revealed, and all flesh shall see it together;" when "they shall not hurt nor destroy in all God's holy mountain;" when "the earth shall be filled with the knowledge of the Lord, as the waters cover the sea." But this period is not to be ushered in as many of our spiritual guides teach,* by the progress of society, or the march of intellect, or the advancement of science; not by the spread of modern opinions, or the rise and growth of liberal institutions; nor by means of schools, and hospitals, and peace societies, and temperance societies; no, nor even by means of Sunday schools, and tract societies, and missions to the heathen, however good in their places these may be (and we have reason to thank God in many respects for them): It is not by these means that Satan's kingdom will be overthrown—that the world will be delivered from his dire oppression, and the universal reign of righteousness be introduced; *but by the coming of our Lord Jesus Christ from heaven.*

---

* Witness the declarations of Henry Ward Beecher, David Swing, H. W. Thomas, Robert Collyer, and other influential ministers who entertain this view.

And this is the one grand event placed before us in the "more sure word of prophecy"—an event which men have contrived, indeed, to put off to an indefinitely distant period, but which in Scripture is ever represented as the one impending event, placed as such before both saints and sinners.

Men have taught that this event is certainly at the distance of a thousand years. But Christ says, "Of that day and hour knoweth no man, no, not the angels of heaven, but my Father only."

One consideration that can hardly fail to have weight with those who really value God's Word, is the very large proportion of it which is occupied with prophetic subjects. From Isaiah to Malachi, all is prophecy; to say nothing of a great deal in preceding portions, such as Jacob's prophecy in Genesis—those of Moses in Leviticus and Deuteronomy—as well as numerous passages in the books of Samuel, the Kings, and the Chronicles. A great part of the Psalms, too, are prophetic in their character.

Then, as to the New Testament itself, one entire book—the closing one—is prophecy. We have prophecies in the epistles of Jude, James, and Peter. Paul's notable prophecy in his second epistle to the Thessalonians is well known, besides others in his other epistles. And as to the gospels, which of them is there that contains no prophecy? Matt. xiii., xxiv., and xxv.; Mark xiii.; Luke xxi.; and John xiv.-xvi., are the chief prophecies of the great prophet, our Lord Jesus Christ himself. And do we well to turn aside from these, as from writings of little (if any) interest or moment to us? Should we deem such conduct in a child commendable, or the reverse? Suppose he should receive a long letter from an absent parent, a great part of which is devoted to the child's instruction on a certain class of subjects, what should we think of his conduct, if he hastily passed over the whole of this, scarcely reading it at all, to pay exclusive attention to some parts of the letter, which, for some reason or other, he preferred? Would he be honoring his father by such a course? And are we honoring our Father, who has graciously caused the Holy Scriptures to be written, by neglecting, as many do, the prophetic portions of them?

Some say that the study of prophecy is merely speculative. But this is untrue. All anticipations of the future drawn from any other source are mere speculations. Those actually drawn from the prophetic Word of God are sober realities, certain facts. And as to its not being practical, as some allege, the truth is, there is nothing more so.

There are two objections, however, on which it may be well to bestow a little attention. One is, the extravagancies into which, as it is alleged, many have been led by directing their attention to unfulfilled prophecy. We are told of the Anabaptists, and Fifth Monarchy-men of a by-gone age; we are told of Southcote, of Irving, and of the Mormonites of the present day. We are told of these, and warned against all attempts to study prophecy, by the fearful errors into which these parties have fallen. But let us look at this objection. If it proves anything at all, it proves too much. We are not to study prophecy, we are told, because fanatical misguided men have made bad use of it. But if the abuse of anything be a good argument against the use of it, it is not from prophetic Scripture alone that we must turn aside, but from the whole Word of God. What Scripture is there that has not been perverted by misguided men, or wilful deceivers, to purposes of evil? Then, besides, all or nearly all those who are held up as beacons to warn us against the study of prophecy pretended to have received new revelations themselves. *They set up to be prophets.* It is not the sober, serious, patient, prayerful study of what is already revealed in God's Word that characterizes fanatical teachers on prophecy; but the pretension to having themselves received new revelations. It is not that we wish you to be prophets, or wish you to receive anything that any one pretending to be a prophet would teach you. It is to guard you against all such delusions that we invite you to render your most serious attention to the teaching of the prophetic pages of God's holy Word. And the fact is, that the objection we are considering, not only proves too much for the objectors, but also proves the very opposite of what it is brought to prove. Instead of proving that prophecy should be neglected, it proves that it should be studied; calmly indeed, with prayer—in entire dependence upon the Spirit of God, but still studied. What is it that gives such deceivers as have been referred to the fearful power they possess? It is the ignorance—the wide-spread ignorance—of professing Christians on the subjects those deceivers dilate upon. Where is it that a man is most liable to be led astray? In the path he continually treads—a path with every step of which he is as familiar as with his own fireside? No; the night may be very dark, and the path very intricate; but he knows too well to be in it led astray. It is in some unknown region, where every path and every lane is new to him, and where darkness moreover settles and broods over the entire scene. It is there that the *ignis fatuus* leads the traveller into a bog, or a false treacherous guide conducts him, through winding paths, into a den of thieves. And so with the Word of God. It is not by means of those parts with which we are best acquainted, that Satan and his emissaries succeed in leading us astray. But if there be any large field of truth with which men are not conversant; some large tract of Scripture consigned, as the prophetic parts are generally, to oblivion and neglect; there it is that the tempter puts forth his skill. By calling attention to some striking part of these neglected portions, he arouses the attention of neglectful multitudes, and makes them feel how ignorant they have been; and they do actually come to see some truths which they have not seen before. But alas! it is only that these truths are used by Satan as his gilded bait to disguise the concealed hook of some deadly error, which he contrives to hide amid the long neglected and now apparently recovered truth. It is the neglect of the Word of God that throws the door open to the enemy. It is the neglect of the prophetic Word that makes professing Christians the easy prey of any deceiver who pretends to prophetic light. The Lord grant us to take warning by the past. Having our loins girt about with truth, and taking the words of the Spirit, which is the Word of God, may we be kept from all the wiles of the devil; may we be enabled to withstand in the evil day, and having done all, may we stand.

But there is another objection more subtile, and perhaps with a certain class more influential than the one we have been considering. It is this. It is alleged that the *chief*, if not the *only*, use of prophecy is after the event, to demonstrate the truth of God, and evince his faithfulness in fulfilling his word. It is said, "Ah, but you cannot understand prophecy till after the occurrence of the event it foretells. This is the only key by which it can be unlocked, and then it will be seen how God has spoken, and has fulfilled his word. But it is of no use examining prophecy till then." Such is the objection. That fulfilled prophecy has the use affirmed, one would not, of course, think of denying.

Fulfilled prophecy has this use undoubtedly. But to say of *unfulfilled* prophecy, that its chief use is after the event is to go directly in the face of the plainest declarations of God's word. See 2 Peter i. 19; "We have also a more sure word of prophecy, whereunto ye do well to take heed." When? When the events have been accomplished, and the light thus shed upon the prophecy makes plain that God has spoken the truth? Is that the time? No; "whereunto ye do well that ye take heed, *as unto a light that shineth in a dark place,* UNTIL the day dawn, and the day star arise in your hearts."* The use of prophecy is that of a lamp, to light the traveller's feet along the dark and dreary path. It is not intended for a candle to be held up to the sun, to make it manifest that the sun shines at noonday. As some one has in substance, remarked, if the chief use of unfulfilled prophecy be after the event, it must be either to the righteous or to the wicked that it is thus useful. It cannot be to the wicked; it is too late to be of use to them, when its predictions have been accomplished in their destruction. The flood proved the truth of God's word by Noah; but it was too late to be of any advantage to the guilty world, who perished for not having heeded the warning before. And as to the righteous, sure-

---

* Or rather, "until the (Millennial) day dawn, and the day star (Christ) arise. In your hearts knowing this first," etc. It does not refer to conversion, as many have supposed, but to a period prophesied of, beyond the "until" season.

ly they don't need the fulfilment of prophecy to satisfy them that God speaks the truth. *We are not Christians unless we do believe this.* No, dear reader, we do not need prophecy to be fulfilled, in order to certify us of the truth of God. But we do need all the light it sheds upon our present path, and upon the whole scene around, to guide us through its intricate mazes to that city of habitation which it reveals to us as the home of our weary hearts, and our eternal dwelling-place of joy.

Were attention more generally given to the manner in which prophecy has hitherto received its accomplishment, we may easily believe that there would be more correct opinions formed of a large portion of scripture, now perverted at will by multitudes whose interpretations have not the slightest regard to the language of the text. It is thus that expositions, as various as they are fanciful, are put upon the most obvious declarations of God's word, the meaning of which it would be almost impossible to miss, did we not prefer our own wisdom in discovering some hidden sense, or in substituting our own notions, rather than study to ascertain the mind of the Holy Spirit.

In maintaining the literal fulfilment of prophecy, we are not, however, to be understood as denying that the prophetic scriptures contain many *figures*, which are only to be explained as figurative language should always be. We only ask in behalf of divine predictions, the same principle of interpretation that is extended to other compositions, inspired as well as uninspired. The occasional introduction of figures in the gospels or epistles, for example, is never advanced as a warrant for departure from the principle of literal interpretation as the ordinary mode of determining their meaning or of ascertaining their objects. Thus, although the apostle Paul speaks of the posterity of Abraham (Rom. xi. 17-24) *under the figure* of "branches broken off," and to be yet again "*graffed* into their own *olive tree*," no one imagines that the use of such a figure forms a reason for denying that the *literal Israel* is there meant.

Yet such is the very treatment given to the Old Testament prophecies, concerning which many seem to consider themselves as not only at liberty to make anything or everything of the figures they contain, but even to use the plain unfigured predictions in a manner precisely similar. Thus, by the system of spiritualizing, statements the most definite and precise have attributed to them a vagueness which leaves every man the right of putting upon them whatever meaning his inclination or his fancy may suggest. Fidelity to the Word of God surely requires, that where figures do *not* occur, figurative interpretations be *not* introduced; and where figures *are* employed, that they be really interpreted as such, and not as something to be fashioned at our pleasure, without regard to the end for which they are given.

In every case, except that of interpreting God's word, it would be considered as the highest injustice to an author to change entirely the meaning of the language ordinarily employed, simply because figures occasionally occurred; nor would any one consider himself warranted to interpret even the figures themselves otherwise than in consistency with the connecting statements given, discriminating the one from the other. Yet without the least pretence to *Divine authority* for the principle, statements in scripture, given wholly or partially in unfigured language, are equally subjected to the spiritualizing process, and meanings extracted which nothing less than a *new revelation* could enable the reader to discover; or rather, it may be said, which *of themselves* constitute a new revelation, having never been *in* the written language of these statements, to be in any way elicited from it.

In endeavoring to ascertain the meaning of scripture prophecy, it is important to observe, that, from the very nature of most of its predictions, they are only susceptible of a literal interpretation. Were scripture readers to attend with care to the context, and even to circumstances introduced in the various prophecies sometimes spiritualized, they would find in these alone, checks sufficient to prevent such a perversion of their meaning and design. But it is also farther to be observed, that to explain away all the predictions concerning the glory of Christ, is to justify his rejection by the Jews, notwithstanding of the plain declarations of his humility and sufferings. For, if we are at liberty to spiritualize all the prophecies which foretell his reign in glory, how can we blame them for adopting a similar mode of interpreting other predictions not more clear and far less numerous?

Besides, this is a method of interpretation which seems not only repugnant to reason, but is quite inconsistent with that literal fulfilment which prophecy has hitherto received. If all past predictions, except where figures are obviously used, have had their fulfilment *literally*, even when the minuteness of prophecy was extreme, on what principle of interpretation is a mode of fulfilment yet unprecedented now to be expected? We can point to a long series of predictions which have been literally fulfilled, and to others which are being so at this very day, in their utmost minutiæ, and can see no reason to suppose that those which, for aught we can tell, may relate to the ensuing month, or the ensuing year, are not to have a literal fulfilment also, as no intimation is given by the spirit of prophecy of any period at which this mode of their accomplishment shall cease. Thus alone, indeed, can the criterion divinely given, by which to distinguish the *true* from the *false* prophet, be of any avail: "If thou say in thine heart, How shall we know the word which the Lord hath *not* spoken? When a prophet speaketh in the name of the Lord, *if the thing follow not* nor come to pass, that is the thing which the Lord hath not spoken, but the prophet hath spoken it presumptuously" (Deut. xxvii. 21, 22). And the minuteness with which Prophecy has hitherto been fulfilled, proves how safely the rule may be applied. The past dealings of God in this respect—which show the perfect correspondence between the prediction and its accomplishment—have however been much neglected; and hence, perhaps, the unwillingness so often displayed believingly to receive the promises he has bestowed, without the intervention of our limitations; and hence also, our unbelieving fears to submit Divine predictions concerning the future to the ordeal which Jehovah himself has prescribed.

In conclusion then, let us remember that prophecy is not designed to furnish food for curious imaginations, or a field for the exercise of intellectual power. It is addressed to faith, to be by it simply received as God's word, and thus to become incorporated with the very existence of the inner man, humbling us at God's feet, weaning us from the world, enabling us alike to despise its attractions, and to be quiet and peaceful amid its convulsions and its overturns, knowing beforehand what will be the end of its vaunting, proud career, and how God has prepared for the safety and blessing of his own—some *above* and others *amid* the widespread, general crash.

Опечатки:

На с. 60 следует читать «Сионских» вместо «Слонских»

На с. 75 следует читать «Рис. 3» вместо «Рис. 2» и «Рис. 4» вместо «Рис. 3»

CHAPTER II.

THE ISRAELITES, AS RELATED TO PROPHECY IN THE PAST.

Having shown, as we trust, the importance of prophetic study, if we would be enlightened relative to events yet future ; and having shown also that the only way to understand the prophets is to take them at their word, literally, except where figures are obviously used, we now proceed a step farther and assert that the history and destiny of all nations who have been made the subject of prophecy is so interwoven with that of the nation of Israel that the two cannot well be separated. In fact, so important a place does Israel occupy among the nations in the estimation of God, that even in the days of Peleg (several generations before Abraham), "when the Most High divided to the nations their inheritance, when he separated the sons of Adam, he set the bounds of the people according to the number of the children of Israel" (Gen. x. 25). That which formed the central and controlling thought in his arrangements was his foreknowledge of the number of the children of Israel. Israel was dear to him above all the other nations—"His portion, and the lot of his inheritance." The nations were to be both placed and governed in relation to Israel; and hence in this primary appointment of the bounds or limits of their respective dominions, all was settled with reference to Israel. Could anything more emphatically declare the pre-eminent place which Israel occupies in Divine counsels touching this earth—its government—and its inhabitants.

In consequence of God having made Israel the centre of his earthly government, we find that even the profane history of nations centres round it. "Egypt, Assyria, Babylon, Persia, Greece, Rome, all contend for Israel's land, are known in connexion with it, or actually get their full imperial possession and character at the time they acquired possession of it—we do not say *by gaining possession of it*—but at the epoch at which they did. Though clouds of dark traditions, scarce pierced by modern researches, hang over all the rest of the nations, and obscure their history while revealing their existence, in the neighborhood of Israel all is light. The light of Israel's history is shed on all around them. It is preserved almost with modern accuracy, when a few fragments scarce rescue from entire oblivion other ancient histories. We have to disentomb the remains of the Thebes and the Ninevehs to get at the history of their ancient monarchs, and to know their dynasties; while, by God's providence, that which gives some historic data to the glories of Mizraim and Ashur, confirms in its detail that of which we have already the minutest particulars in Israel's authentic history. We find. in pictures yet fresh on the lore-covered walls of the country of the Pharaohs, the very kinds of overseers over the Jews making their bricks, of which Moses speaks in the books of Exodus. Modern research alone has given the place and importance to those countries which the scriptures had already assigned them."

In the purposes of God then, Israel occupies a central point, around which all other nations revolve. This may seem strange to some, in view of the fact that Israel's land has been so long a wilderness, her cities a heap of ruins, and herself in captivity, whilst other nations have been exalted far above her, ruling her with impunity. Yet even this condition of affairs is but another proof of the truth of our proposition. God raised up these Gentile powers and temporarily transferred to their keeping his people Israel, who on account of their sinfulness had wearied his patience, and secured his displeasure. As a punishment then he gave them into captivity, but not an unending one. Far from it. In the meantime therefore, the history of Israel is cotemporaneous with that of his captors, and oppressors. And if we would learn what the destiny of existing nations shall be, we must first learn what God's purposes are relative to Israel in the future. It seems to be a settled law that Israel's humiliation shall result in Gentile exaltation, but Israel's exaltation in Gentile humiliation. When Israel, as a nation, were in favor with God, he blessed them abundantly, and subdued all the nations round about to their will. But when Israel rebelled against him, he exalted their enemies far above them, and as a consequence Israel has been sorely despised and persecuted, and the pride and power of the Gentiles has known no bounds.

This state of things will cease; in short, it will be reversed. Israel, we shall find is destined to recover their lost estate, and take rank once more among the nations of earth as the head and not the tail. But more of this hereafter.

Having shown how closely the history and destiny of the nations is interwoven with that of Israel, the reader will readily perceive the importance of first getting a clear scriptural idea of God's future purposes relative to this ancient people, and of the land he gave to their fathers. This, coupled with such prophecies as we can find relative to Gentile powers, will lead us to a correct solution of the Eastern question.

As a preparatory step then, we must glance rapidly at the past history of this wonderful people, and learn how perfectly the Word of God has received its accomplishment during the season of their great chastisement.

We need not recount God's dealings with them in their deliverance from Egyptian bondage, nor the many deliverances he wrought out for them afterwards. We need not relate to you the flourishing state of their kingdom under David and Solomon, nor how the nation became divided under Rehoboam, ten of the tribes organizing a separate kingdom under Jeroboam. This is history familiar to all who have but a smattering of Bible knowledge.

Passing on then, we will introduce the predictions of Moses concerning the future destiny of Israel as recorded in Deut. xxviii. After recounting the blessings that would come upon them in case of obedience, he proceeded to relate a series of curses which would surely overtake them in case of their disobedience. Among other things he says, "The stranger that is within thee shall get up above thee very high; and thou shalt come down *very low*. He shall lend to thee, and thou shalt not lend to him; he shall be the head, and thou shalt be the tail." He also declares that the Lord should "scatter them among all people, from one end of the earth even unto the other . . . and among these nations shalt thou find *no ease*, neither shall the sole of thy foot have rest; but the Lord shall give thee there a trembling heart, and failing of eyes, and sorrow of mind: and thy life shall hang in doubt before thee, and thou shalt fear day and night, and shalt have none assurance of thy life: in the morning thou shalt say, Would God it were even! and at even thou shalt say, Would God it were morning! for the fear of thine heart wherewith thou shalt fear, and for the sight of thine eyes, which thou shalt see."

In order that we may realize how literally these fearful predictions have been fulfilled let us briefly trace the history of this people, recalling some of the most prominent persecutions that have overtaken them.

In the days of Shalmanezer, king of Assyria, God gave up the ten tribes who had previously revolted, into the hands of this Gentile king, who carried them into captivity, from which they have never returned.

About 134 years after this, Nebuchadnezzar, king of Babylon, overthrew the kingdom of Judah, slew the king's sons, the chief priest, and all the nobility, together with a multitude of others who were reckoned as the principal and official persons of the kingdom. The remainder were carried captive to Babylon. Thus in darkness and in blood the sun of David's kingdom set. Ezekiel, a prophet of that time, referring to this great overthrow says, "Thus saith the Lord God, Remove the diadem, and take off the crown; this shall not be the same: exalt him that is low, and abase him that is high. I will overturn, overturn, overturn it, and it shall be no more until he come whose right it is: and I will give it him" (Ezek. xxi. 26, 27). Thus clearly foretelling the abasement of Zedekiah, the last king of David's line that ever sat on David's throne, and also predicting the continued overturning of the royal kingdom and diadem until the coming of Him "whose right it is," (see Luke i. 32, 33) even Jesus, to whom it should eventually be given.

The appointed term of their seventy years captivity being ended, Ezra and Nehemiah led the people back again to Jerusalem, rebuilt its walls and gates, and erected also a temple for the worship of the Most High God. But God's judgments again overtook them, for in the days of Antiochus Epiphanes (B. C. 166) their city was abandoned to the fury of the Syrian army for three days, during which time over 40,000 persons were slain, and nearly an equal number sold for slaves. The impious monarch also forced his way into the temple, and even penetrated into the holy place; tore off the golden ornaments, carried away the sacred treasures and utensils, and in order to offer the greatest insult to the Jewish religion, sacrificed a large hog on the altar of burnt offering.

About two years subsequent to this, Antiochus despatched Appollonius, governor of Syria, at the head of twenty-two thousand men, commanding him to destroy Jerusalem, massacre the men, and sell the women and children for slaves. The king's officer waited until the sabbath day, when the people were assembled for the solemn worship of God, when he executed his horrid commands with unrelenting barbarity. The city was plundered, set on fire, and its walls demolished.

Not yet satiated with blood, this cruel persecutor issued an edict to the effect that all within his dominions should worship no gods but those of the king. The statue of Jupiter Olympus was set up on the altar of burnt offering, and all who refused to offer their adorations were either massacred, or compelled to endure the most exquisite tortures. The king himself visited the city of Jerusalem in order to personally superintend the execution of his decrees.

At a later period (B. C. 65) the Jews were visited by a Roman army, during which over twelve thousand persons were slain, and many perished by suicide. Subsequently, Herod, a stranger and Idumean, ascended the throne of Judea, and proved to be a most cruel and relentless tyrant. He caused many to be put to death, and exhibited a marked contempt for the Jewish religion and laws. He it was who caused the children of Bethlehem to be slain in expectation of cutting off Jesus the new born king. The next great judgment that overtook this doomed nation was that which occurred A. D. 70, when Titus, the Roman general, surrounded the city of Jerusalem with his legions, and after a long seige captured and destroyed it. It is estimated that 1,100,000 Jews perished at this time.

About sixty years subsequent to this great overthrow, one Bar-Chochab (son of a star) arose, and was accepted by the nation as the Messiah. Vast armies followed his leadership, but met with final defeat, some 580,000 Jews perishing by the sword, and multitudes more being sold into slavery.

In Persia, (A. D. 200) Sapor, the king, commenced a violent persecution against them, which was incited by the jealousy of his subjects.

Mahomet, (A. D. 612) after flattering them awhile, finally became their inveterate foe, and turning his arms against them slew vast multitudes, drove them into exile, confiscated their estates, and compelled all who remained to pay the most exhorbitant tribute.

During the disputes respecting image worship in the eighth century, such as would not bow to the cross and images were subjected to the greatest vexations. In 1055, the king of Grenada became so incensed against them that 100,000 families were reduced to the greatest extremities. During the eleventh and twelfth centuries, the Jews suffered the greatest indignities from the Crusaders, who trampled upon them, extorted their money, and put them to death, on their march to and from the Holy Land.

In the first crusade, 1500 were massacred at Strasburg, 1300 at Mayence, and 1200 were slain in Batavia. Women at Treves, seeing the Crusaders approach, killed their children, preferring this to having them fall into the hands of the Crusaders. When Jerusalem was taken, all the Jews were inhumanly murdered. In England, in 1189, when Richard I. ascended the throne, the mob fell upon them, and put multitudes to death. From Henry III. they purchased an edict to preserve them from the outrages of the Crusaders. Some of the archbishops and bishops forbade any one's selling them provisions on pain of ex-communication. They were often accused of the foulest crimes, and though not found guilty, were compelled to pay the most enormous fines. Seven hundred were massacred in London in 1262, by the barons, to please the Londoners. King Edward I. passed many severe enactments against them, and drew from them several hundred thousand pounds. In 1287 he ordered all the Jews in the kingdom to be imprisoned and 280 to be executed in London, besides vast numbers in other cities; and in 1290 he ordered them all to be banished from the kingdom, never to return under pain of death. He seized their whole property, scarcely allowing them sufficient to bear their expences into other lands; the number expelled was 16,511. From this time they were shut out of England for 350 years.

In France, under Louis IX., they were sold with the land on which they dwelt, and in the year 1238, during a violent persecution, 2500 Jews were put to death under the most cruel tortures. Soon after, they were all banished by Louis, from his dominions. They were recalled and then banished many times from that country.

In Italy, Pope John XXII., pretending that they affronted the holy cross, ordered their banishment from his territories, but recalled the edict for 100,000 florins.

The sufferings of the Jews in Spain, from the Crusaders, were probably greater than in any part of Europe. Their own writers indeed view them greater than their people were ever called to suffer since the destruction of Jerusalem. In Spain, too, they were accused of poisoning the rivers and wells, and 15,000 were in consequence put to death. In Spain the officers of the Inquisition brought about a terrible result upon the Jews, in which 2,000 were put to death, many were long imprisoned, and such as had their liberty were compelled to wear two red crosses on their garments, to show that they had escaped from the flames; 17,000 returned to the bosom of the Papal Church. In 1412, 16,000 Jews were forced to profess Popery. About 1472 they were barbarously massacred in the dominions of Venice. In 1472, Ferdinand and Isabella issued a fatal edict, which banished all the Jews, in four months, from Spain; 70,000 families, or 800,000 persons, pursuant to this decree, left that beautiful kingdom amidst the greatest distress and suffering. Vast multitudes perished on their way to foreign countries. Such as reached them were in the deepest distress, and many perished from famine and disease before they could find a settled abode. In Lisbon many fell a prey to the Inquisition. At Mentz, in Germany, 12,000 were killed on a charge of poisoning the fountains. In 1350, Louis, king of Hungary, banished them all from his dominions.

The Jews, by an invasion of the Tartars in 1291, were driven from place to place, and robbed of their possessions. And during the wars of Tamerlane, in 1500, all their schools were broken up, their learned men destroyed, and the whole people exceedingly impoverished. In Persia they suffered in 1666, under

Shah Abbas II., a general massacre for three years. All, without distinction of age or sex, were destroyed without pity, who would not renounce their religion. The negroes in Africa have been found treating them also in the most contemptuous manner, calling them dogs. In the city of Nuremberg, they were not permitted to walk without a guide. At Augsburg they were suffered to enter only at the price of a florin for every hour they wished to remain. In Frankfort, where they numbered some 30,000, they were plundered and ridiculed, and shut up in one long narrow street, which was closed upon then at both ends, every night during divine service among others. In Prague, where they filled a third part of the city, they were exposed to the greatest insults and confined to the most degrading employments. By the popes of the sixteenth century they were treated with great severity. Pius V. expelled them in 1569 from every part of the dominions, except Rome and Ancona. The Jews offered Charles V. 800,000 crowns of gold if he would suffer them to return to Spain; but their offer was rejected. In Spain and Portugal they lived only by dissimulating. Outwardly they were good Catholics, while they secretly practiced the Mosaic rites, and if at any time they were discovered they were at once put to the tortures of the Inquisition. The sufferings of the Jews in that horrid tribunal for three centuries, were beyond all description. In Holland, a fine of 1,000 florins was laid on the Jew who found the least fault with the government. In the Ottoman Empire they have ever been treated with the utmost contempt, paying a tax for the privilege of worshipping in their own way. In their ancient city of Jerusalem, they have for 1800 years received nothing but oppression, ignominy and reproach. Sometimes they have for ages been entirely excluded from it, and not suffered to look at it from the distant mountains, and when permitted to reside there, have exhibited the most affecting spectacle of human wretchedness.

To peruse details attending the numerous persecutions of this people had we space to give them, would chill the blood of every reader. God's word concerning them has been literally fulfilled in the oft repeated cry of His people in the midst of their distresses—" Would God it were even!" or " Would God it were morning!" No rest have they had for the soles of their feet, but instead, they have been exiles and wanderers, suffering the utmost contempt and cruel persecutions of every nation on the face of the earth. Yet, strange to say, amid all these sufferings they have preserved the worship of the God of Israel, rejecting the vagaries and idolatry of Paganism, Romanism, and other superstitions, at the expense of their lives. And although decree after decree has been issued for their extermination as a people, yet here they are, in the midst of all nations, speaking their languages, adopting many of their customs, but remaining still a distinct people. Whilst other nations have been lost, and their individuality gone, yet the Hebrew nation still lives, a monument of God's miraculous power, and an evidence of the truth of His word concerning them.

Whatever prejudices men may entertain towards them, yet candor will compel them to admit that of all the nations of the earth, the Jewish nation has unquestionably been the largest blessing to the human race. However much any nation may have been indebted to other nations, for arts and for science, for genius and for eloquence, for taste and for civilization, for riches or for jurisprudence, to the Jews all nations are indebted for a better light than the wisest of the heathen ever could discern, or the most enlightened of their philosophers ever did or could bestow. All Divine knowledge on that which most nearly concerns us, respecting our Maker or ourselves, our duty now and our happiness forever, and that spiritual light which the most favored human beings enjoy at this moment, God has vouchsafed to bestow through the Jewish prophets, Jewish evangelists and Jewish apostles. Our Lord himself, according to the flesh, was born of a Jewish mother, and lived and suffered, and wrought his mighty miracles, and died and rose again in Judea. Our daily spiritual food, and our richest inheritance of blessing came through this nation. Those churches which first adorned Christianity with unequalled piety and beauty, sprang up in Judea; and through their lively faith and ardent love, the Gospel of Christ speedily spread through the Roman Empire, and so has reached every Christian heart.

God has preserved this wonderful nation for a purpose. He has rich blessings in store for them. The cup of bitterness which they have drank will soon be taken from them and passed over to the lips of those who have so willingly persecuted them. It will, indeed, prove to be "a cup of trembling" to them, but they will be made to drink it nevertheless. Isaiah li. 17--23.

For a number of years past, there have been unusual movements among this people, and among the nations concerning them. There is a growing interest manifested in their future welfare. Politicians even are beginning to speculate relative to the possibility of their restoration to the land of their fathers. The yoke which has so long borne them down has been lightened in some cases, and entirely removed in others. On every hand there are unmistakable signs of great changes, so that were we to judge merely from a human standpoint, we might almost predict with certainty a complete revolution in Jewish affairs. But we are not left to speculation. We have the positive word of God to guide us, so that we may speak with certainty. Hence, students of the prophetic word, unlike politicians and others, wait not for the events predicted to near their fulfilment ere they declare their faith in them, but hundreds of years previous, when everything seems unpropitious from a human standpoint, they declare with confidence, what shall come to pass, basing their declarations entirely upon the unfailing word of God.

Having traced the hand of God as shown in the past history of Israel, it will be our purpose next to introduce the testimony of the prophets and apostles as to their future, preparatory to learning what shall be the fate of the nations who become entangled in Israel's affairs.

CHAPTER III.

THE ISRAELITES AS RELATED TO PROPHECY IN THE FUTURE.

That the great bulk of the Israelitish race will yet be converted to Christ the Messiah, and be again grafted upon the olive tree of the spiritual Israel from which they have been broken off, is well agreed on all hands. Whitby says, "This hath been the constant doctrine of the Church of Christ, owned by the Greek and Latin fathers, and by all the commentators I have met with." The inspired declarations upon this subject are too explicit to be evaded. "*All Israel shall be saved:* as it is written, There shall come out of Sion the Deliverer, and shall *turn away ungodliness from Jacob:* FOR THIS IS MY COVENANT UNTO THEM."

That the scattered family of Jacob shall again be gathered, and nationally restored to the land of their fathers, is not very generally admitted. Some have no patience with such a theory, and sneeringly ask, What can be the object of such a restoration? What end is it to answer? What purpose can it subserve? For our own part we are heartily willing to acquiesce in any arrangements the blessed Savior may make; and we will at the same time persist in holding as the truth of God whatsoever we find clearly stated in his holy word, no matter where it may lead us.

The first passage in the New Testament to which we refer is one uttered by the Savior himself, where he says, "Jerusalem shall be trodden down of the Gentiles, until the times of the Gentiles be fulfilled." Take a plain common-sense view of this passage, and what does it mean? The treading down of Jerusalem can be nothing more nor less than the destruction and desolation of the Jewish metropolis and state by the deportation of the Jewish people? And what is the cessation of this treading down of the Jewish metropolis and state but the restoration of the Jewish people? Who can make anything else out of it?

A second New Testament passage on the subject is that which we have already quoted, where Paul says, "All Israel shall be saved, as it is written, There shall come out of Sion the Deliverer, and shall turn away ungodliness from Jacob." This is generally understood as a spiritual salvation by conversion to Messiah. And a spiritual deliverance is certainly a prominent and controlling idea in the passage. It is expressly stated that one feature is the removal of ungodliness. But this interpretation by no means exhausts the passage. It has an appendage in the succeeding verse which throws much additional light and consequence upon the predicted deliverance. Paul says that this salvation is just what was included in God's ancient covenant with the Jewish fathers. "All Israel shall be saved, for this is God's covenant unto them when he shall take away their sins." *

In relation to this covenant of God with the fathers, we take the broad ground, and no man can overturn it, that it has never yet been even nearly fulfilled. Its great fullness is still matter of promise, to be verified hereafter, when Christ shall "come a second time unto salvation." That covenant charters to them the land from the river of Egypt to the great river Euphrates, for their everlasting possession ; which has never yet been made good. That covenant guarantees unto them a national existence and glory as lasting as the great orbs of heaven, which yet remains to be fulfilled. Wherever the terms of that covenant are given, from first to last these are two of its prominent and immutable features. And if "all Israel is to be saved," according to that covenant which Paul explicitly declares to be unchangeable,—or "without repentance,"—it is demonstrated to an absolute certainty that they will yet be gathered and replaced in that "goodly land and large" in which they dwelt when David controlled their triumphant armies, and Solomon and his court were the admiration of the world.

A third reference to this subject in the New Testament is contained in the first of Acts, where the

---

* For a more complete record of the covenant alluded to, read Gen. xv. 18-21; xvii. 4-8; xxvi. 3-5; xlviii. 3, 4.

disciples put to the Savior their last question:—
"Lord, wilt thou at this time restore the kingdom to Israel?" What did they mean by that inquiry? Every preacher, commentator and thoughtful Bible-reader will tell you that the Jews looked for the Messiah as a reigning prince. For many years they had been a dependent and oppressed people. In the period of the Savior's stay on earth, they were subject to the dominion of the Cæsars. And their great hope was, that when Christ came he would judge their oppressors, deliver them from their national dejection, and restore their state and kingdom to former independence and glory. The disciples shared in the common expectation. Hence their despondency at his crucifixion, saying, "We trusted that it had been he which should have redeemed Israel." They felt all their fond hopes crushed in the Savior's death. But as soon as he arose from the dead and reappeared among them, their old hopes revived, and they looked anew for the Messiah's deliverance of their nation. And this was the burden of their question as here presented. They wished to know if Christ was then about to effect the expected national redemption, and "restore the kingdom to Israel." The question then arises. Were their anticipations respecting this redemption right or wrong? We maintain that they were right. If they were not right, then we are at a loss to account for the fact that these anticipations retained their full force through three

or four years of special daily instruction from the Savior himself, and continued uppermost in their minds to the very last moment of Christ's stay upon earth. Then again, if they were all this while cherishing erroneous expectations in this matter, would not the Savior have set them right now that he was at the point of leaving them until his final "coming and kingdom?" But look at his answer. Not one word did he utter against the views implied in their question. All he said was, "It is not for you to know the times and seasons which the Father hath put in his own power." They did not ask him whether he would restore the kingdom to Israel; they took all that as settled; and the Savior answered them upon the same assumption. They simply wished to know whether that was the time, and the answer was that they were not to know the time. As regards everything but the time, the reply leaves it just as it was apprehended by the inquirers. And, taking the circumstances and all together, it is to us perfectly conclusive that it is the Divine intention to "restore the kingdom to Israel" in the exact sense in which the disciples expected it; and that the blessed Savior, in his last words, meant to throw his solemn sanction upon the hope of Israel's restoration. We have no interest in forcing or perverting the scriptures from their plain and obvious meaning, and if we did not solemnly believe what we here state we would not utter it.

A fourth allusion which the New Testament contains upon this subject, is in the fifteenth of Acts, where James says, "Simeon hath declared how God at the first did visit the Gentiles, to take out of them a people for his name. And to this agree the words of the prophets, as it is written, After this I will return, and will build again the tabernacle of David which is fallen down; and I will build again the ruins thereof, and I will set it up: that the residue of men might seek after the Lord, and all the Gentiles, upon whom my name is called, saith the Lord."

Two things are here to be specially noted. The first is the object of the present dispensation; which is, to take out of the Gentiles a people for God's name. There is nothing in the scriptures to warrant the hope that the world is to be converted before Christ comes the second time. The whole object of the present economy is, to take out from among men a people for the Lord. This is here pointedly declared. But James goes further. He assures us that it is the purpose of God, as announced by the prophets, to return after the object of this dispensation has been attained, and then to "build again the tabernacle of David which is fallen down." And in order to understand what is meant by this rebuilding of David's tabernacle, we need only revert to the original prophecy in the ninth of Amos, which treats of Israel's dispersion for their sins, and their redemption in the latter days, " that they may possess the remnant of Edom, and of all the Gentiles, and be pulled out of their land no more." Surely the matter is as plain as words can make it, that, at the end of this dispensation, Christ will come and restore the scattered Jews to their own land, and reign over the house of Jacob forever upon the throne of his father David.

Although there are still other allusions to this subject in the New Testament, yet it is more especially in the Old Testament that we are to seek the amplest details of Israel's hopes. That is peculiarly the gospel of the Jews. The prophecies there on record respecting the conversion and restoration of Jacob's seed may well be pronounced by Bishop Newton to be innumerable. There is hardly a chapter from Psalms to Malachi which does not in some way bear upon it. To give all we would have to recite about half of all that the prophets have written.

Let us refer you to a few specimens: "Thus saith the Lord: Behold, I will take the children of Israel from among the Gentiles, whither they be gone, and will gather them on every side, and bring them into their own land." What could be plainer than this? It is useless to say that it refers to the deliverance from Babylon; for this prediction relates to "the whole house of Israel," whilst only parts of Judah and Benjamin ever returned from the Babylonian captivity. The restoration here predicted is to be attended with the everlasting reunion of the two wings of the great Israelitish schism, so that they shall "not be divided into two kingdoms any more at all;" which to this day has not taken place. This restoration is to be perpetual, "forever;" the restoration from Babylon was only temporary. This restoration is to be attended with the ultimate entire conversion of the whole nation, and an everlasting release from all their filthiness and sins; but they have involved themselves deeper in crime since they came back from Babylon than before, and even slew the Messiah.

Neither will it answer to say that the restoration here predicted is to be understood spiritually, as referring to the final conversion of the Jewish people, and their incorporation into the Christian church. The church is no more their land than it is the land of Gentile believers. The prophecy sets forth their spiritual renovation in words sufficiently plain to need no further spiritualizing; thus leaving us to infer that the other particulars are to be understood in the same plain and obvious sense. The prophecy also contains a promise of the multiplication of man and beast, which certainly cannot apply to the church unless our sanctuaries are yet to be filled with the brute creation. The same prophecy promises to Israel their old estates,—"I will settle them after their old estates,"—which, whether taken in a spiritual or a literal sense, necessarily implies their restoration to a condition of isolation and distinctness from all other orders or races of men. But this is not all. If the regathering and restoration of the Jewish people into their own land is to be understood spiritually, then their deportation from that land and dispersion must be understood spiritually too. The one must correspond to the other. The same prediction contains both sides, in the same strain of discourse; and the promise of the restoration is founded on the predicate of their previous dispersion. Hence, if the one is spiritual, the other is equally spiritual; and if the one is literal and outward, so also must the other be. God himself, speaking upon this very subject, has settled this point forever. "It shall come to pass, that *like as* I have watched over them to pluck up, and to break down, and to destroy, and to afflict; so will I watch over them to build, and to plant, saith the Lord" (Jer. xxxi. 28). Here then, we take our stand with unflinching firmness, and upon the immutable basis of God's own word, demand of all opponents either to show that the spoiling was only spiritual, or else admit that their final restoration is to be national and literal. If Titus only took the church, and not the literal city,—if he only cast the Jews out of the church, and did not kill them or carry them away captives,—if he did not devastate and depopulate Palestine, but only intercepted God's spiritual blessings by desolating the ways to eternal life,— *then*, but *only* then, can this promised regathering of Israel into their own land be interpreted so as to preclude their national restoration. "I will gather them," saith God, "and bring them into their own land."

The same literal restoration of the exiled descendants of Jacob is foretold by Moses, in his farewell address to that people. We there have a graphic delineation of the whole history of Israel up to the present and still future times. Moses there foretells a sore and wide dispersion; but he predicts with equal explicitness a final and complete recovery from it. "The Lord thy God will turn thy captivity, and have compassion upon thee, and will gather thee from all the nations whither the Lord thy God hath scattered thee. If any of thine be driven out unto the uttermost parts of heaven, from thence will the Lord thy God fetch thee: and the Lord thy God will bring thee into the land which thy fathers possessed, and thou shalt possess it: and he will multiply thee above thy fathers:" (Deut. xxx.) Never, to this day, has there occurred to Israel such a deliverance, from such a dispersion. And the idea that this prediction is to be fulfilled by the simple incorporation of the Jews into the existing church, is worse than ridiculous. They are, therefore to be restored.*

Reader, what you think of these things, we know

---

* In further pursuit of the testimony upon this inexhaustible subject read Jer. xxxii. 37-42: Ezek. xxxiv. 22-31; xxxvii. 21-28; Amos ix. 11-15: Micah iv. 6, 7: Zeph. iii. 14-20: Zech. viii. 7, 8, 14, 20-23, and scores of other testimonies.

not; but we are fully persuaded that it is God's immutable purpose to bring back the Jewish race to its ancient home. The passages which we have given more than prove it; whilst the great mass of prophecy upon the subject has not been touched. And if even all these solemn statements of God were to pass for nothing, the simple but significant facts of history furnish ground enough upon which to infer that Israel is yet to be restored to that land where Abraham lived and the Savior died.

Look at that wonderful race! For nearly two thousand years, scattered all over the face of the earth, oppressed, despised, persecuted, unmercifully butchered; yet still existing, as distinct in manners, feelings and hopes, as when Moses was their leader and Aaron was their priest. Since God shook them out of their ancient dwelling-places, nations, thrones, kingdoms, have risen, flourished, fallen, and lost their proud subjects in the ever-varying stream of human affairs; but Israel still stands apart, unshaken by earth's mutations, with the accents of David and Isaiah still upon their lips, and still looking for the promised Shiloh to take them back in triumph to their father-land. The Christian church herself, glorious as she is in her list of martyrs and attirements of grace and truth, has, since then, been depressed, diminished, enfeebled, by violence and defections which she has found it hard to survive; but the house of Jacob, with all their wrongs and spoliations, have only strengthened with their trials, whilst all the bitterness of their great cup of sorrow has never made them forget that they were Hebrews, or loosened the tenacity with which they cling to God's peculiar covenant unto them. Kings have issued severe edicts and commissioned bloody executions against them, and the seditious and spiteful multitudes have afflicted them with outrages still more violent and tragical. Princes and people, civilized and savage, Pagans, Mahometans, and professing Christians, disagreeing in so many things, have more than once made common cause for their extermination. But still they live and thrive. Though for nearly twenty centuries without a temple, prophet, king, country, or home, they still bear the same marks which characterized them before Vespasian set foot on their sacred land or Titus invested their loved Jerusalem.

Look, again, at their holy city. "Captured, ravaged, burnt, razed to the foundation, dispeopled, its deported citizens sold into slavery, and forbidden by severest penalties to visit their native seats;" yet, even in its mournful desolations, it stands forth, a thing to itself, and altogether distinguished from all other ruins. Who now weeps over the fall of Troy? What people pays pilgrimages of devotion to the ruin-piles of mighty Nineveh or Babylon? These great monuments of human pride and glory sleep their last sleep, and no tear falls upon their unhonored graves. But Jerusalem, even in her ashes, is still dear to the hearts of millions, and the mere mention of that name awakens pangs of mingled grief and hope as deep as those that weighed upon her captive sons when they mourned under the willows by Babel's waters. Beautifully has it been said, that ever and anon, and from all the winds of heaven, Zion's exiled children come to visit her, and with eyes weeping sore, bewail her widowhood. No city was ever honored thus. None else thus receives pilgrimages from the fiftieth generation of its outcast population. None but this, after centuries of such dispersion, could, at the first call, gather beneath its wings the whole of its wide-wandering family. None but this has possessed a spell sufficient to keep its people still distinct, even in remotest regions, and in the face of the mightiest inducements. And none but itself can now be re-peopled with precisely the same race which left it nearly two thousand years ago."

Now, what mean these anomalous, we might say, miraculous facts? Why are the Jewish people still distinct, and Jerusalem's walls still dear as ever? Meet a Jew where you will, he is a mere wanderer or sojourner, in a position to move at the shortest warning. Scattered over all lands beneath the sun, he has never taken permanent root in any. And of all that have ever tried to fix themselves in the Holy Land,—Romans and Persians, Saracens and Turks, Egyptian Caliphs and Latin Christians; Mamelukes and Ottomans,—none have ever been able to gain a permanent foothold in it. Why is all this? Men of political science may try their skill at explanation; but after all the problem will reduce itself to this: that God has his own settled purpose with this people and this place, holding the one in reserve for the other until each shall be forever satisfied with its own. Here history is prophecy. And if all the holy seers were silent, the very stones themselves cry out for Israel's restoration. The rocks of Palestine will have no lord but Jacob.

We are, therefore, prepared to adopt the statement of David N. Lord, a very profound and able American expositor of sacred prophecy, that "those who assent to the true laws of language and symbols will no more deny or doubt that the prophecies teach that the Israelites are to be restored, than those who assent to the definitions and axioms of geometry will deny the demonstrations that are founded on them. There is not a proposition in the whole circle of human knowledge of more perfect certainty than that God has revealed the purpose of regathering that scattered nation, establishing them as his chosen people, and reappointing a temple-worship at Jerusalem that is to embrace some of their ancient rites. It is not merely certain, but is taught with a frequency, an emphasis and an amplitude, and invested with a dignity and grandeur that are proportionable to the vastness and wonderfulness of the measure in the great scheme of his administration over the world."

The return of this people will doubtless begin, in a small way, under what some will call the natural course of things. There are even now already thousands of Jews in Jerusalem and its vicinity. A goodly portion of the Holy Land is said to be at this moment under mortgages in the hands of those rich Jewish bankers, the Rothschilds, of Europe. The effects of the peace concluded in 1856, between the great powers of the Old World, in securing toleration of other religions under the Turkish laws, was merely a signal for the downfall of the Ottoman empire, and the opening of the door for Israel's return. Many religious associations in all parts of Protestant Christendom have since been in efficient operation with and for the Jews, all looking more or less to their ultimate restoration. These things, all working in the line of Israel's intense desires, cannot but work mighty consequences. They are the preliminaries of the second Jewish exodus.

But it is not by these alone that Israel shall be redeemed. According to the eighteenth of Isaiah, and other passages, there will yet be great national movements upon the subject. We there read of a great maritime power, spreading wide its wings, existing somewhere in the Far West from Palestine, and which must either be the United States, Great Britain, or perhaps both, as one in religion, language and laws. This power, accustomed to send messengers by sea, is to become interested in behalf of the Jews, and to aid them with contributions, embassies, treaty-stipulations, fleets and other ways. The prophet himself calls to this power, (we use Horseley's translation,) "Ho! land spreading wide the shadow of thy wings! Go, as a swift messenger, to a people wonderful from the beginning hitherto, a nation expecting, expecting, and trampled under foot, whose land rivers (invading armies) have spoiled; and all the inhabitants of the world, and dwellers upon earth, shall see the lifting up, as it were, of a banner upon the mountains; and shall hear the sounding, as it were, of a trumpet." That is, as we understand it, when these movements in favor of the Jews begin, there will be an extraordinary waking up upon the subject, and a very deep interest felt, so that men generally will regard themselves as specially called to help in the great work. And it is a singular fact, in this connection, that the United States government, without any assignable cause for it, did, only a few years ago, send out Lieut. Lynch and his party, to explore the Jordan and obtain detailed and authentic descriptions of the condition and topography of Israel's land. England has done the same, as if these countries, so closely allied in so many particulars, were already laying the foundations for their work and mission in bringing back the dispersed children of Abraham.

We have no expectation that anything very decisive or extraordinary will occur in the line of the

Jewish restoration, until God's judgments shall begin to tear asunder the nations. When the "distress of nations with perplexity" shall have fully set in, and the day of earth's troubles has come, then the people of Israel shall flock home, like doves to their windows; and the Lord himself shall show wonders in their favor, like to the day that he brought them up out of Egypt. See Isa. lx.

The accompaniments and great results of this final restoration of the Jewish people are so wonderful and miraculous, that it is hardly possible for us to form a proper conception of them. Not many years from this present time, perhaps the whole story will be told. One thing is certain, that Israel's restoration is not for Israel alone, but for the whole world. It is one of those means, in the wonderful arrangements of God, for letting forth his mercy and salvation upon all the inhabitants of the earth. It is in the seed of Abraham that all nations shall be blessed. Israel's restoration shall be the world's resurrection. In the language of Hamilton, "The moment the veil is rent from Israel's eyes, the vail will be rent from a thousand prophecies; and, read in the light of restored and regenerated Judah, the word of God will sparkle with unwonted coruscations, and, like deep-colored gems that look dusty in cloud light, many of its dark sayings will brighten up into its divinest truths when the beams break forth from Salem."

Nor need you be surprised, dear reader, when,

in the light of the prophecies, we declare the conviction that Jerusalem is yet to become the metropolis of the world, just as it was the metropolis of Judea in the days of Solomon. All the nations of this world are yet to come under one universal government—the kingdom of Christ and his glorified saints. "God hath highly exalted him, and given him a name that is above every name; that at the name of Jesus every knee should bow, and every tongue confess that Jesus Christ is Lord:" (Phil. ii. 10.) "Now we see not yet all things put under him:" (Heb. ii. 8.) But "he must reign until he hath put all enemies under his feet:" (1 Cor. xv. 25.) "The Gentiles must be given him as his inheritance, and the uttermost parts of the earth for his possession:" (Psa. ii. 8.) He has declared himself to be appointed King of the Jews, and Prince of the kings of the earth: (Matt. xxvii. 11; Rev. i. 5.) "The kingdoms of the world are to become the kingdoms of our Lord and his Christ; and he shall reign forever and ever:" (Rev. xi. 15.) And the centre and seat of this great kingdom is Jerusalem. "The Lord of hosts shall reign"—where?—"in Mount Zion, and in Jerusalem, and before his ancients gloriously:" (Isa. xxiv. 23.) The Lord also shall roar"—from whence?—"out of Zion, and utter his voice from Jerusalem, and the heavens and the earth shall shake; but the Lord will be the hope of his people, and the strength of the children of Israel. So shall ye know that I am the Lord your God, dwelling in Zion, my holy mountain: then shall Jerusalem be holy:" (Joel iii. 16, 17.) Nay, as there is to be a literal reign of the Son of man on earth, where is it most likely that his imperial seat will be? What locality does the mind most naturally turn to? The holy associations and the very geographical position of Palestine mark it out with signal felicity as the place where the Son of Mary shall hold his sublime court. As remarked by one who has looked carefully at the matter, "Palestine is so remarkably situated, that it forms the bridge between two continents and a gateway to a third. Were the population and wealth of Europe, Asia and Africa condensed into single points, Palestine would be the centre of their common gravity. And with the amazing facilities of modern intercourse, and the prodigious extent of modern traffic, it is not easy to estimate the commercial grandeur to which a kingdom may attain, placed as it were on the very apex of the old world, with its three continents spreading out beneath its feet, and with the Red Sea on one side to bring it all the golden treasures and spicy harvests of the East, and the Mediterranean floating in on the other side all the skill and enterprise and knowledge of the West. For the sake of higher ends it seems the purpose of God to make the Holy Land a mart of nations, and by bringing the forces of the Gentiles to Jerusalem, to send the blessing of Abraham over all the earth."

It is also well known that ever since the Jews

first entered Canaan, it has been the battle ground of nations. To this hour it is mixed up with the mightiest disputes that disturb the world. The Assyrian, the Egyptian and the Roman of old, the Arab, the Turk, the Greek, the Papist and the Rabbi of our times, all have claimed it as if the earth contained not another prize like it. The Russian war, which converted the Crimea into a Golgotha and made the world tremble, had its beginning in Jerusalem, in hot disputes and altercations about its shrines and holy places. And the history of the world is filled with illustrations of the desirableness that has ever adhered to that "goodly land," and of the interests involved in its occupation. Divine prophecy, too, sounded through the long galleries of centuries, proclaims the fact that all the nations shall yet be governed from that point.

> "The day is coming—yea, is now at hand—
>   When wars shall struggle on the Syrian plains,—
> Wars, such as ne'er have been on earth,
>   Nor the sun seen in all his ancient reigns;—
> The day is coming—yea, is now at hand—
>   When urged by heaven, to her old hallowed ground
> Shall sweet Solyma lead back her tribes,
>   While with sweet tones her Hebrew camps resound.
> Then shall stand still Euphrates; then shall stop,
>   In fierce affright, Niles many-founted river,
> Then, too, with whirl gigantic, shall the way
>   Of the Red Sea cleave wide apart and sever.
> Day of revival! then shall festal Zion
>   To her eternal God build shrine on shrine,—
> High Lebanon and Hermon shout with singing,
>   While flowering olives crown their cliffs divine!"

CHAPTER IV.

THE EASTERN QUESTION.

In view of what we have already presented, it will be manifest to the most casual reader, that before the events there enumerated can take place, great changes must be effected in relation to the Jews—the Holy Land—and the power that has so long held sway there—Turkey. That these changes are already in progress is also plain. In fact it is nothing more nor less than the gradual unfolding of the purposes of God concerning the restoration of Israel and the subsequent blessing of all nations, that has given rise in late years to that problem of problems, known as "The Eastern Question!" The secular press of the entire world has teemed with articles and telegrams relative to this all-absorbing theme; yet, even now, there are thousands of intelligent readers who are unacquainted with the real points at issue.

If we would learn what the Eastern Question really is, and should venture to ask the great powers of Europe, whose diplomats have racked their brains for fifty years past, in their vain efforts to solve its intricate problems ; or seek to know from Rome, St. Petersburg and Constantinople, the great

centres of Catholicism and Mohammedanism, or
England, the representative of Protestantism, we
should probably hear them reply that it was one of
the greatest questions of the day ; in short, that no
question of such magnitude has presented itself for
adjustment since the days when Napoleon overran
Europe, and threatened to become master of the
world.

The Eastern Question is one that involves the
destiny of empires and kingdoms. Its solution is
one that will witness the change of boundary lines
of kingdoms, the creation of new governments, and
a general remodeling of the map of both Europe and
Asia. It is the knowledge of this fact that has
postponed the final settlement so long. A glance
at the map of these continents as they are now divided, will enable anyone to see the situation at
once. Turkey, an empire stretching from the Persian Empire in the East to the Adriatic Sea in the
West, and the Austrian Empire on the North to the
African coast on the South, is a prize, the distribution of which must necessarily create intense anxiety among the governments interested.

Again, it is not simply a territorial question, but
a religious one also. This great empire, binding
as it does, two continents together, and controlling
the very key to the wealth and commercial interests
of the world, is made up of a heterogeneous population, representing various kinds of religious faith.
Aside from those who profess Mohammedanism,

which is the religion of the empire, there are millions of Greek Catholics, whose spiritual head and recognized protector, is the Czar of Russia. Such an element as this, scattered mostly through European Turkey, has necessarily produced a constant tendency toward dissolution. It is manifest that this could not be otherwise when we remember that there has not only been a disposition on the part of these crushed millions to appeal to their spiritual head for release and protection, but there has been a like disposition on his part to grant it. Indeed, it is the knowledge of this fact, that has kept the great powers of Europe in such an agony of suspense for so long a time. It is this that has given rise to so many conferences, wars, and treaties, for the purpose of maintaining "the integrity of the Ottoman Empire." It was the dread of Russian ambition, and the fear of what might ensue, were the time ever to come for the dissolution of the decaying Turkish power, that led to the intervention of England and her allies in 1840, to check the ambition of Egypt, who, but for this, would doubtless have gained Constantinople. Again, in 1853-5, England, France, and Sardinia joined hands to drive Russia back, after she had set out to protect the Holy Places at Jerusalem; an interference which resulted in the signing of the Treaty of Paris, by which the Black Sea was neutralized. In 1860, a French army and an English fleet again interfered to terminate the conflict between the Druses and

Maronites, after fearful massacres of Christians at Damascus, and in the Lebanon. In short, the wise statesmen of Europe have exerted themselves to the utmost (as witness the six months conference of the six great powers in 1876-7,) to prevent a conflict which might involve the destiny of this politically-weak, but territorially-important Empire, but all in vain. The hand-writing on the wall long since declared its doom, and no one has comprehended it more fully than the Turks themselves. They speak only of their *kismet*, or doom. Bishop Southgate, and other travelers in Turkey, tell us that they repeatedly heard such words as these : " We are no longer Mussulmans—the Mussulman sabre is broken—the Osmanlees will be driven out of Europe by the Ghiaours, and driven through Asia to the regions from which they first sprang. It is *kismet!* We cannot resist destiny !"

In view of the continual growth of Russia, and her settled policy, for nigh two hundred years past, to humiliate Turkey ; and in view of the gradual waning of the Turkish crescent during the same period, it was manifest that the time should come when a collision would ensue that would materially advance the settlement of the Eastern Question. Kossuth foresaw this when he remarked " In Turkey will be decided the fate of the world." Napoleon I., also, when languishing upon the island of St. Helena, predicted the future conquest of Turkey by Russia. Addressing Governor Hudson, he said :

"In the natural course of events, Turkey must fall to Russia. The greatest part of her people are Greeks, who, you may say, are Russians. The powers it would injure are England, France, Austria, and Prussia. As to Austria, it will be very easy for Russia to engage her assistance by giving her Servia, and other provinces bordering upon the Austrian dominions reaching near Constantinople. The only hypothesis that ever France and England may be allied with sincerity will be in order to prevent this. But even this will not avail. France, England and Prussia, united, cannot prevent it. Once mistress of Constantinople, Russia gets all the commerce of the Mediterranean, becomes a great naval power, and God knows then what may happen. She quarrels with you and marches off an army to India of 70,000 good soldiers, and 100,000 Cossacks, which to her is nothing, and England loses India. All this I foresaw. I see further into futurity than others, and I wanted to establish a barrier against those barbarians by re-establishing the kingdom of Poland and putting Poniatowski at its head, but you *imbeciles* of ministers would not consent. A hundred years hence I shall be praised, and Europe, especially England, will lament that I did not succeed. When they see the fairest countries in Europe overrun, and a prey to northern barbarians, they will say *Napoleon was right!*

Alexander II., also, the present Emperor of Russia, upon ascending the throne, indicated his determination to adhere to the policy of his family in these words : "May Providence so aid us that we may be able to strengthen Russia in the higher degree of power and glory; that by us may be accomplished the *views and designs of our illustrious predecessors*, Peter, Catherine, Alexander, and our august father, of imperishable memory."

From this it will be seen that, dating from the days of Peter the Great, there has existed a distinct line of policy in the Russian government, and that each successor to the throne has endeavored, as nearly as circumstances would admit, to adhere to it. What this policy is will best be learned from a perusal of

THE FAMOUS WILL OF PETER THE GREAT.

In the name of the Holy and Indivisible Trinity, we, Peter the First to all our descendants and successors to the throne and Government of the Russian nation:

Having by the great God of whom we received our existence, been also endowed with the gift of prescience, we view the Russians as called, in the course of future events, to the general dominion of Europe.

This opinion is founded on the fact, that the other European nations have reached a state of old age next to caducity, toward which they are journeying with giant strides; hence it follows, that they should easily and undoubtedly be conquered by a people young and new, when it shall have acquired its strength and vigor. We view the invasion of the East and West countries by the North as a periodical movement, decreed among the arcana of that Providence that regenerated the Roman people through the invasion of the barbarians.

The emigrations of the polar men are like the flood of the Nile which comes at certain periods to fertilize the exhausted lands of Egypt. We found Russia a rivulet, and leave it converted into a river;

THE DESTINY OF RUSSIA.

and my successors will find it a sea, destined to fertilize impoverished Europe, and its waves will break down all opposing dykes, if my descendants have but the wisdom to direct the current.

To this end I leave the following instructions, which are recommended to their attention, and constant observance.

1. To have the Russian nation constantly at war, that the soldiery may be always disciplined and ready for action. Allow the nation no rest, but for the replenishing of the treasury, reorganizing the armies, and choosing the opportune moment for attack; making in this manner, peace serve war, and war serve peace, in the interests, aggrandizement and prosperity of Russia.

2. To attract, by all possible means, the most efficient and celebrated military officers in Europe, during war, and the highly educated, scientific men of all countries, in time of peace, that the Russians may enjoy the advantages of other countries, without losing their own identity.

3. To take part, on all occasions, in the disputes and contentions among the states of Europe, especially those of Germany, in which, as the nearest, we are the most directly interested.

4. To subdue Poland; foment their continual rivalries and disturbances; gain their nobles by bribery; influence their diets, and by intrigue, take action in the election of their kings; form partisan cliques, and for their protection, send them Muscovite troops, to remain in the country until the moment of complete occupation. If the neighboring powers make opposition, quiet them at once by dismembering the country, and giving each a part.

5. To take what we can from Sweden, and make any attack by her, a pretense for subjugation. To effect this, separate her from Denmark, and likewise Denmark from Sweden, and foment with care, all animosities and rivalries between them.

6. To select wives for the Russian princes among the princesses of Germany, for the multiplying of family alliances will conciliate interests, and by them unite Germany to our cause, and increase our influence in that country.

7. To attend assiduously to forming an alliance with England, for our commerce; the assistance of that power we most need, for the building up of a maritime force, and she will be of the greatest ser-

vice in supplying us with her gold, in exchange for our lumber and other productions. Continual intercourse with her merchants and sailors will accustom ours to navigation and commerce.

8. Extend ourselves unceasingly toward the North, the whole length of the Baltic, and likewise to the South by the Black Sea.

9. To take every possible means of gaining Constantinople and the Indies, (for he who rules there will be the true sovereign of the world); excite war continually in Turkey and Persia; establish fortresses in the Black Sea; get control of the sea by degrees, and also of the Baltic, which is a double point, necessary to the realization of our project; accelerate as much as possible, the decay of Persia; penetrate to the Persian Gulf—re-establish, if possible, by the way of Syria, the ancient commerce of the Levant; advance to the Indies, which are the great depot of the world. Once there we can do without the gold of England.

10. Obtain and carefully cultivate the alliance of Austria; support (apparently) her ideas of future dominion over Germany; excite animosities and rivalries among her princes—thus causing each party to claim the assistance of Russia, and exercise over this country a species of protection that will prepare for future dominion.

11. Interest the House of Austria in the expulsion of the Turks from Europe, and quiet their dissensions at the moment of the conquest of Constantinople, (having excited war among the old states of Europe), by giving to Austria a portion of the conquest, which afterwards will or can be reclaimed.

12. Unite within your borders all the disunited or schismatic Greeks now scattered in Hungary and Poland, making ourselves their centre, establishing beforehand an independent church by a species of autocracy and sacerdotal supremacy.

13. Sweden dismembered, Persia subdued, Poland subjected, and Turkey conquered, our armies united, and the Black and the Baltic Seas guarded by our ships of war, it will be necessary to propose separately, and with the greatest secrecy, to the Court of Versailles, and afterwards to that of Vienna, to divide with them the empire of the universe.

If one of the two accept this offer, so flattering to their ambition and self-love, let her serve to annihilate the other, commencing a contest, the issue of which cannot be doubtful; and Russia may take possession of all the East and a great part of Europe.

If both nations should refuse the offer made by Russia, (which is not at all probable), it will be necessary to excite quarrels among them, which will engage them in a war with each other. Then Russia, improving the decisive moment, advances her troops (assembled beforehand) on France and Germany at the same time. Two squadrons proceed—one by the Sea of Azof, and the other by the port of Archangel—filled with Asiatic hordes, under the convoy of our armed ships in the Black Sea and the Baltic. Advance by the Mediterranean and the ocean, inundate France on one side, while Germany is inundated on the other, and these two countries conquered, the rest of Europe will pass under the yoke without firing a gun. Thus may and should be effected the subjugation of Europe.

In view of all the various complications connected with the Eastern Question, we may say that it is really a "Europero-Africo-Asiatic Question," seeing that it is a question that involves the future interests of "three continents, three seas, four oceans, seven empires, and especially of the Mediterranean kingdoms, regencies, and principalities. The fall of the Turkish Empire has for some time past been accepted by the statesmen of Europe as a foregone conclusion, and it has also been admitted that the war which should be waged in consequence would result in the entire re-apportionment of Europe and a part of Asia, erasing the landmarks of ten centuries, as thoroughly as those of the old Roman Pagan Empire under the irruption of the Goths, the Vandals and the Huns, or the overthrow of Eastern Christendom under the banners of Mohammed II. and Solyman the Magnificent.

The Eastern Question, however, in its present phase, presents but a preparatory step towards the final outcome. It was necessary that Turkey should be weakened and humiliated, in order that her hold upon the Holy Land should be slackened, if not entirely relinquished. For some years past we have seen one concession after another made at the instance of Christian nations, granting privileges in that country to Jews and others such as would have resulted in death formerly, if indulged in. Thus, step by step has the way been prepared for the return of Israel to their own land. And not only has Turkey removed many of her grievous burdens from the necks of this oppressed race, but all countries have done the same, until to-day we see the Jews exercising in most civilized countries equal priviliges with other citizens. A complete revolution in their favor has been wrought within a generation. Everything tends to show that the time to favor Zion is near, yea, very near. And we regard this last contest of Russia with Turkey as another evidence. The hands of every power were seemingly tied until the Northern Avenger thoroughly chastised the Turkish Power. And we may be sure of one thing, that in the end some arrangement will be effected whereby the Holy Land will be freed from the tyranny of the Turk, and Israel will be at liberty to return under ample protection, to the land of his fathers. That this will be accomplished we are certain, even though

Jewish Infidels may be found in this country who scoff at the mere mention of their nation returning to the Promised Land. God's word cannot be broken and he has said it. And that this is the expectation of the great mass of the Jewish people is well-known. May God speed the day when their hopes shall be realized, for with it will come better days for this sin-cursed earth of ours.

The final settlement of the much-talked-of Eastern Question, however, will not be left for human wisdom or human prowess to adjust. Neither will it be finally settled in Turkey proper, but as foreshown by the prophets of God, it will be on the mountains of Israel. There it will be definitely and forever settled by the interposition of a Higher power, even One from Heaven. The prophets of God have clearly foretold this great event, and it remains therefore for those who believe that the Word of the Lord cannot be broken, to stand still and see the wonderful workings of Almighty Power, as one event after another leads on to the last grand conflict in that land of all lands—Palestine.

CHAPTER V.

AN UNFULFILLED PROPHECY OF EZEKIEL.

In the 38th and 39th chapters of Ezekiel we find a most remarkable prophecy concerning the Jews and their enemies, a prophecy that has never received its fulfilment, and upon which we base our belief as to the destiny of Russia and other powers who will be allied with her as there shown.

Seeing that all our readers are possessed of King James' Version, we thought best not to occupy our space with a repetition of the prophecy as there translated, but instead, we give it as recorded in a copy of the Scriptures translated by Isaac Leeser,* an Israelite in faith and by birth also. We shall also place in foot-notes certain variations as shown in the Septuagint and Douay Versions,† so that our readers may have the benefit of them all in reaching their own conclusions as to what the prophecy really signifies.

---

* " The twenty-four books of the Holy Scriptures; carefully translated according to the Massoretic Text, after the best Jewish authorities, by Isaac Leeser. Philadelphia: Published at 1227 Walnut street. 5617 " (A. D. 1857).

† The readings from the Septuagint Version will be marked "S. V." and those from the Douay, "D. V."

THE PROPHECY CONCERNING RUSSIA AND OTHER POWERS.

1 ¶ And the word of the Lord came unto me, saying,

2 Son of man, direct thy face against Gog of the land of Magog, the prince of Rosh, Meshech and Thubal, and prophesy against him,

3 And say, Thus hath said the Lord Eternal, Behold, I will be against thee, O Gog, the prince of Rosh, Meshech and Thubal;

4 And I will derange thee, and put hooks in thy jaws,[1] and I will bring thee forth, and all thy army, horses and horsemen, all of them clothed in elegant attire, a great assemblage with bucklers and shields, all of them grasping swords.

5 Persia, Cush, and Put (shall be) with them; all of them with shield and helmet;

6 Gomer and all of its armies; the house of Thogarmah out of the farthest north, and all its armies: many people shall be with thee.

7 Be thou ready, and prepare thyself, thou, and all thy assemblages that are assembled about thee, and be thou a guard unto them.[2]

8 After many days shalt thou be ordered forward; in the end of years shalt thou come into the land that is recovering from the sword, and is gathered together out of many people, against the mountains of Israel, which have been ruined for a very long time:[3] (to a people) that are brought forth out of the nations, and that now dwell in safety, all of them.

9 Thou wilt ascend and come like a tempest, like a cloud to cover the earth wilt thou be, thou, and all thy armies, and the many people with thee.

10 ¶ Thus hath said the Lord Eternal, It will also come to pass, at the same time, that things will come into thy mind, and thou wilt entertain an evil device;[4]

11 And thou wilt say, I will go up over the land of open towns; I will come against those that are careless, that dwell in safety, all of whom dwell without walls, and have neither bars nor gates,

12 To snatch up the spoil, and to take away the prey; to turn thy

---

1. *D. V.* "And I will turn thee about, and I will put a bit in thy jaws."
2. *D. V.* "And be Thou commander over them."
3. *S. V.* "Against the land of Israel, which was entirely desolate."
4. *D. V.* "In that day projects shall enter into thy heart, and thou shalt conceive a mischievous design."

hand against the ruined places now inhabited, and against the people that are gathered out of the nations, that have gotten cattle and goods, that dwell in the highest part of the land.⁵

13 Sheba, and Dedan, and the traders of Tharshish, with all her young lions, will say unto thee, Art thou come to plunder the spoil? hast thou gathered thy company to carry off the prey? to bear away silver and gold, to take away cattle and goods, to plunder a great spoil?⁶

14 Therefore, prophesy, son of man, and say unto Gog, Thus hath said the Lord Eternal, Behold, on the day when my people of Israel dwelleth in safety, shalt thou know (my power).⁷

15 And thou wilt come from thy place out of the farthest ends of the north, thou, and many people with thee, all of them riding upon horses, a great assemblage, and a mighty army;

16 And thou wilt come up against my people of Israel, like a cloud to cover the land; in the latter days will this be,⁸ and I will bring thee over my land, in order that the nations may know me, when I am sanctified on thee, before their eyes, O Gog.

17 ¶ Thus hath said the Lord Eternal, Art thou (not) he of whom I have spoken in ancient days through means of my servants the prophets of Israel, who prophesied in those days (many) years, that I would bring thee against them?

18 And it shall come to pass at the same time, on the day of Gog's coming over the land of Israel, saith the Lord Eternal, that my fury shall be kindled in my nose.

19 And in my zealousness, in the fire of my wrath, have I spoken,

---

5. *D. V.* "to lay thy hand upon them that have been wasted, and afterwards restored, and upon the people that is gathered together out of the nations, which hath begun to possess and to dwell in the midst of the earth." *S. V.* "against a nation that is gathered from many nations, that have acquired property, dwelling in the midst of the land."

6. *S. V.* "They are come for plunder to take a prey, and to get spoils; thou hast gathered thy multitude to take silver and gold, to carry off property, to take spoils."

7. *S. V.* "Wilt not thou arise in that day, when my people Israel are dwelling securely, and come out of the place from the farthest north."

8. *D. V.* "Shalt be in the latter days." *S. V.* "it shall come to pass in the last days."

Surely on that day there shall be a great earthquake in the country of Israel;[9]

20 And there shall quake at my presence the fishes of the sea, and the fowls of the heaven, and the beasts of the field, and every creeping thing that creepeth upon the earth, and all the men that are upon the face of the earth, and the mountains shall be thrown down, and the cliffs shall fall, and every wall shall fall to the ground.

21 And I will call against him throughout all my mountains for the sword, saith the Lord Eternal: every man's sword shall be against his brother.[10]

22 And I will hold judgment over him with pestilence and with blood (-shedding); and an overflowing rain, and great hailstones, fire and sulphur will I let rain over him and his armies, and over the many people that are with him.[11]

23 Thus will I magnify myself, and sanctify myself, and make myself known before the eyes of many nations: and they shall know that I am the Lord.

---

1 ¶ But thou, O son of man, prophesy against Gog, and say, Thus hath said the Lord Eternal, Behold, I will be against thee, O Gog, the prince of Rosh, Meshech and Thubal;[12]

2 And I will derange thee, and lead thee astray, and will cause thee to come up from the farthest ends of the north;[13] and I will bring thee upon the mountains of Israel;

3 And I will strike thy bow out of thy left hand, and thy arrows will I cause to fall out of thy right hand.

---

9. *D. V.* "A great commotion." *S. V.* "A great shaking."
10. *S. V.* "I will summon against it even every fear, says the Lord; the sword of every man shall be against his brother." *D. V.* "Every man's sword shall be pointed against his brother."
11. *S. V.* "I will judge him with pestilence and blood and sweeping rain, and hailstones; and I will rain upon him fire and brimstone, and upon all that are with him. *D. V.* "I will judge him with pestilence and with blood, and with violent rain, and vast hailstones; I will rain fire and brimstone upon him, and upon his army, and upon the many nations that are with him."
12. *S. V.* "O Gog, prince of Rhos, Mesoch, and Thubel."
13. *D. V.* "I will turn thee round, and I will lead thee out, and will make thee go up from the northern parts." *S. V.* "I will assemble thee, and guide thee, and raise thee up on the extremity of the north."

4 Upon the mountains of Israel shalt thou fall, thou, and all thy armies and the people that are with thee: unto the ravenous birds, to every thing that hath wings, and to the beasts of the field, do I give thee for food.

5 Upon the open field shalt thou fall; for I have spoken it, saith the Lord Eternal.

6 And I will send a fire against Magog, and against those that dwell in the isles in safety: [14] and they shall know that I am the LORD.

7 And my holy name will I make known in the midst of my people Israel; and I will not permit my holy name to be profaned any more; and the nations shall know that I am the LORD, Holy in Israel. [15]

8 Behold, it cometh, and it taketh place, saith the Lord Eternal: this is the day whereof I have spoken.

9 And the inhabitants of the cities of Israel shall go forth, and shall burn and make fire for heating of the weapons, and shields and bucklers, of bows and of arrows, and of handstaves, and of spears; and they shall feed with them the fire for seven years;

10 And they shall take no wood out of the field, nor cut down any out of the forests; for with weapons shall they feed the fire: and they shall spoil those that spoiled them, and plunder those that plundered them, saith the Lord Eternal.

11 ¶ And it shall come to pass on that day, that I will give unto Gog a place there for a grave in Israel, the valley where people pass over to the east of the sea; and it shall stop the passengers (from passing): [16] and they shall bury there Gog and all his multitude, and they shall call it The valley of the multitude of Gog [Gay hammon Gog].

12 And the house of Israel shall be burying them, in order to cleanse the land, during seven months.

13 Yea all the people of the land shall bury them; and it shall be to them as a renown on the day that I glorify myself,[17] saith the Lord Eternal.

14 And men constantly devoted to this shall they set apart to pass

---

14. *S. V.* "I will send a fire upon Gog, and the islands shall be securely inhabited."
15. *S. V.* "The Holy One in Israel."
16. *D. V.* "Which shall cause astonishment in them that pass by."
17. *D. V.* "It shall be to them a noted day, wherein I was glorified."

through the land, to bury with those that pass through those that remain upon the face of the earth, to cleanse it: at the end of seven months shall they make a search.

15 And those that thus travel will pass through the land; and when any one seeth a human bone, then will he set up a sign by it, till the buriers have buried it in the valley of the multitude of Gog.

16 And also the name of the city shall be Hamonah.[18] Thus shall they cleanse the land.

17 ¶ And thou, O son of man, thus hath said the Lord Eternal, Say unto the birds, to everything that hath wings, and to every beast of the field, Assemble yourselves, and come; gather yourselves from every side to my sacrifice that I do slaughter for you, as a great sacrifice upon the mountains of Israel, that ye may eat flesh, and drink blood.

18 The flesh of the mighty shall ye eat, and the blood of the princes of the earth shall ye drink,—wethers, lambs, and he-goats, bullocks, fatlings of Bashan are they all of them.

19 And ye shall eat fat till ye be sated, and ye shall drink blood till ye be drunken, from my sacrifice which I have slaughtered for you.

20 And ye shall be sated at my table on horses and chariot-teams, on mighty men, and on all men of war,[19] saith the Lord Eternal.

21 And I will display my glory among the nations: and all the nations shall see my punishment that I execute, and my hand that I lay on them.

22 And the house of Israel shall acknowledge that I am the Lord their God from that day and forward.

23 And the nations shall know that for their iniquity did the house of Israel go into exile; because they had trespassed against me, and I had hidden my face from them; and I gave them up therefore into the hand of their oppressors, and they all fell by the sword.

24 According to their uncleanness, and according to their transgressions did I deal with them, and hid my face from them.

25 ¶ Therefore thus hath said the Lord Eternal, Now will I bring back again the captivity of Jacob, and I will have mercy upon the whole house of Israel, and will be zealous for my holy name;

---

18. *S. V.* "Name of the city shall be Burial-place."
19. *D. V.* "With horses, and mighty horsemen, and all the men of war."

26 And they shall feel their disgrace, and all their trespass whereby they had trespassed against me, when they dwelt in their land in safety, with none to make them afraid:

27 When I bring them back again from the people, and gather them out of the land of their enemies, and sanctify myself on them before the eyes of the many nations.

28 And they shall know that I am the Lord their God; because I had exiled them among the nations, but gather them now unto their own land, and leave none of them any more there.

29 And I will not hide my face any more from them; for I will have poured out my spirit over the house of Israel, saith the Lord Eternal.

CHAPTER VI.

IDENTIFICATION OF THE POWERS.

At the commencement of the present war between Russia and Turkey, there were not wanting men who predicted the discomfiture of Russia and the triumph of Turkey. These judged from a human standpoint, believing that other powers would interfere and assist the Turk in his death struggle with the northern giant. Those who were enlightened from a prophetic standpoint however, believed that Russia would triumph, and we may here add that her victories are not yet ended. She is destined to become the greatest power on earth, and to control directly and indirectly vaster armies than the world dreams of. We venture this statement not because we claim superior human wisdom from those around us, but because we have faith unbounded in God's Word. This word *cannot* be broken. Having been sent forth it will not return to him void.

But where is Russia mentioned in God's Word? perhaps you ask. Nowhere, as Russia, but in language unmistakable her future destiny is clearly marked out, as we shall endeavor to show.

It is a well established fact that when the Lord

would make known the future history of any nation or country, he would speak of it as known at the time the prophecy was uttered. To have done otherwise would have resulted in endless confusion. Therefore, if we find nations and countries now existing, named in the Scriptures after their ancient titles, we need not conclude that the prophecy applies to them only as originally known, but that the ancient name adheres to them continually age after age until all that has been predicted concerning them is fulfilled. Hence when God through his prophets reveals beforehand the history of Edom, Moab, Ammon, Tarshish, Pul, Lud, Magog, Meshech, Tubal, Persia, Ethiopia, Libya, Gomer, Togarmah, Sheba, Dedan, Tarshish, and others, he does not change the names of these to suit the various periods of their history, or to harmonize with the changes made by man from time to time, but they remain prophetically the same to the end. Hence if we find that some of these are known in our day as Russia, Africa, Germany, England, etc., we need not stumble on that account, if we find that the prophecies concerning them have never been fulfilled. It matters not to God what men call these prophetic countries in the nineteenth century; to him they remain the same as at first, or when the prophecy concerning them was delivered. With this brief preface we are prepared to examine one of the most remarkable prophecies in God's Word—one that has never been fulfilled, but which is evidently nearing the time when its fulfilment will take place. Indeed, the signs of the times almost warrant us in saying that the present generation may witness its accomplishment even in the remotest detail.

A careful perusal of the prophecy as recorded in our last chapter, will reveal the fact that a great confederacy of nations is spoken of as coming down like a cloud to cover the land of Israel, where will be gathered at that time a people from the nations, that is, an Israelitish people, who will be possessed of wealth, and be dwelling safely in the midst of the land. This great invading host will be thoroughly organized, and possess a leader, who will bring them forward to the mountains of Israel with the intention of possessing themselves of a great spoil, or in other words, of depleting the restored Israelites of their immense wealth which we are told will consist of "silver and gold, cattle and goods." But when this intent becomes manifest by a forward movement of their united armies, an inquiry is instituted by an opposing power, mentioned in the 13th verse of chapter xxxviii. This does not intimidate the aggressor, however, but he presses forward and plants his host on the sacred soil of Palestine, where he meets with a mighty and unlooked for overthrow. Such is a brief outline of this great prophecy.

Before entering into explanatory details we will trace out the various powers named, so as to place beyond doubt who among modern nations are signified. This will necessitate the introduction of more or less extracts from history, and authors who have studied deeply on the subject heretofore, and may not prove to be quite as interesting to the general reader as a mere statement would be, yet we deem it important as a foundation for the building up of our interpretation hereafter.

At the outset of the prophecy Ezekiel is directed to set his face "against Gog, the land of Magog, the chief prince of Meshech and Tubal, and prophesy against him." It is pretty well agreed that the Hebrew words נְשִׂיא רֹאשׁ cannot bear the meaning thus affixed to them. The true reading is "prince of Ros" instead of "the chief prince," and the LXX so render them, (ἄρχοντα ῾Ρως). "Ros," says David Levi, "is not an appellative, as in the common translation of the Bible, but a proper noun." The other sense we are told was adopted by the Vulgate in consequence of the name Rosh not occurring elsewhere in Scripture.

The names communicated to the prophet as taking part in this great event of the latter days are as follows:

1. Gog;
2. Magog;
3. Rosh;
4. Meshech;
5. Tubal;
6. Persia;
7. Ethiopia;
8. Libya;
9. Gomer;
10. Togarmah;
11. Sheba;
12. Dedan;
13. Merchants of Tarshish;
14. The Israelites.

That we may arrive at a correct conclusion concerning each of the parties and countries named, and make no mistake in locating them as known in modern times, we will consider them separately, and in the order named in the prophecy.

Gog.—Boothroyd says that it is generally admitted that Gog was the common name of the kings of Scythia or Tartary, as Pharoah was of the kings of Egypt.

Michaelis compares the word Gog with *Kak* or *Chak*, the general name of kings among the ancient Turks, Moguls, Tartars, Cataians, and Chinese.

Calmet regards Gog as a king of the country or people known as Magog.

Bochart places Gog in the neighborhood of Caucassus. He also derives the name of this celebrated mountain from the Hebrew, Gog-chasan— "the fortress of Gog." There is a fortress in Iberia, to the South of Caucassus, called the Gogarene.

In view of the foregoing opinions, as well as the personal sense in which Ezekiel speaks of Gog, addressing him as a great chieftain, or guard over vast armies of confederate nations, we are safe in saying that Gog, as used in the prophecy under consideration refers to a man—a king, and military leader.

Magog.—This name is applied in the Scriptures both to a person and to a land or people. In Gen. x. 2, Magog appears as the second son of Japheth, in connection with Gomer, and Madai (the Medes). Magog was Gog's original kingdom, although he acquired also Meshech and Tubal.

Simon thinks the name expresses " *augmentation, spreading* of the family."

"The Arabs, it is certain, take *Jiouge* and *Majiouge* for northern nations; and during the last wars of the Russians and Turks they were anxious to be informed on events, expecting, as we learn from Bruce, that they might precede the advent of these northern powers, from which they expect interesting occurrences."—*Wells* in A. D. 1817.

By Josephus, Eustathius, Jerome, Theodoret, and by general consent, Magog is placed North of Tubal, and esteemed as the father of the Scythians on the East and North-east of the Euxine Sea.

Newcome thinks that Magog denotes those vast tracts of country to the North of India and China, which the Greeks called Scythia.

Bagster says that by Magog is probably meant the Scythians or Tartars, called so by Arabian and Syrian writers.

The name Magog, says another writer, would lead us to fix a northern locality. Not only did all the tribes mentioned in connexion with it belong to that quarter, but it is expressly stated by Ezekiel that he was to come up from sides of the North, from a country adjacent to that of Togarmah, or Armenia, and not far from the "isles" or maratime regions of Europe. The people of Magog further appear as having a force of cavalry. The conclusion has been drawn that Magog represents the race of the Scythians. In thus identifying them however, we must not be understood as using the latter term in a strictly ethnographical sense, but as a general expression for the tribes living *North of the Caucasus*. We regard Magog as essentially a *geographical term*, just as it was applied by the Syrians of the middle ages to Asiatic Tartary, and by the Arabians to the district between the Caspian and Euxine seas. The inhabitants of this district in the time of Ezekiel were undoubtedly the people known by the classical name of Scythians.

Houbigant also declares for the Scythians, whose neighbors were the people of Rosh, Meshech and Tubal. Dr. Adam Clark says that several eminent writers espouse this opinion.

"In the Koran Gog and Magog are localized North of the Caucasus. There appears to have been from the earliest times a legend that the enemies of religion and civilization lived in that quarter."—*Hazthansen's Tribes of the Caucasus*, p. 55.

Calmet does not doubt but that the Scythians were from Magog, and confined among the Great and Little Tartars, and perhaps among the Muscovites and other northern people. He says "the Tartars and Muscovites at this day possess the country of the ancient Scythians, and there are still found among them several footsteps of the names

Gog and Magog. They were formerly known as the Mogli."

It is clear from the foregoing testimony that Magog lies north of the Caucasian mountains, and is what is known as the country of the Muscovites and Tartars.

Rosh.—The Scythian Tauri, in the Crimea, were so called, and the Araxes river, in Russia, was also named Rhos. The modern Russians may have assumed this name, as Moscow and Tobolsk from Meshech and Tubal, though their proper ancient name was Slavi or Wends.—*Wells.*

Bagster says the *Rosh* are the Russians, descendents of the ancient inhabitants on the river Araxes, or Rosh.

"The name $P\Omega\Sigma$, *Ros*," says Bochart, in his researches into Sacred Geography, about 1640, "is the most ancient form under which history makes mention of Russia." The Greeks, in the earliest period in which $P\Omega\Sigma$ is mentioned, say $\varepsilon\vartheta\nu o\varsigma\ \delta\varepsilon\ \delta\iota\ P\omega\varsigma\ \Sigma\kappa\upsilon\vartheta\iota\kappa o\nu,\ \pi\varepsilon\rho\iota\ \tau o\upsilon\ \alpha\rho\kappa\tau\omega o\nu\ T\alpha\upsilon\rho o\upsilon$, "the Ros are a Scythian nation, bordering on the Northern Taurus." And their own historians say, "It is related that the Russians (whom the Greeks called $P\omega\varsigma$, *Ros*, and sometimes $P\omega\sigma o\varsigma$, *Rosos*,) derived their name from Ros, a valiant man, who delivered his nation from the yoke of their tyrants."

Meshech.—Calmet says that Meshech was the sixth son of Japhet, and is thought to be the father of the Mosques, a people inhabiting between Iberia and Armenia. Others, he says, believe that the Muscovites are descended from Meshech, which opinion to us seems to be most likely.

Smith's Bible Dictionary says, "Both the name and associations are in favor of the identification of Meshech with the Moschi. The position of the Moschi in the age of Ezekiel was probably the same as is described by Herodotus (iii. 94) viz., on the borders of Colchis and Armenia, where a mountain chain connecting Anti Taurus with Caucasus was named after them the *Moschici Montes*, and where also a district named by the historian Strabo (xi. 477-99) Moschice. In the same neighborhood were the *Tibareni* who have been generally identified with the Biblical *Tubal*. Although the Moschi were comparatively an unimportant race in classical times, they had previously been one of the most powerful nations of Western Asia. The Assyrian monarchs were engaged in frequent wars with them. In the Assyrian inscriptions the name appears under the form of *Mushai*. A similar name, *Moshoash* appears in an Egyptian inscription which commemorates the achievements of the third Rameses. The subsequent history of Meshech is unknown. As far as the name and locality are concerned, Muscovite is a probable hypothesis."

Other writers confirm the outline as given above, concerning Meshech rendering it almost certain that the Muscovites in Russia are the Meshech of to-day. It is also admitted that מֹשִׁי *Mosc*, as it may be spelled without the points, or *Meshech* with them, is the Hebrew name of the people called in modern geography Moscovites. Dr. Newcome says in a note, " Tubal and Meshech, sons of Japheth. The people called Tibareni and Moschi are here meant, who were generally mentioned together, and were situated towards Mount Caucasus." Gesenius styles them " a barbarous people inhabiting the Moschian Mountains between Iberia, Armenia and Colchis."

Tubal.—The fifth son of Japheth, and originally located North of Meshech. Josephus affirms him to be the father of the Asiatic Iberians. Bochart supposes the *Tibareni*, a people mentioned by old authors in this tract, to have been so called from Tubal, by the change of l into r. Meshech and Tubal did originally seat themselves in these tracts, by what is said of these two nations in Ezekiel xxvii. 23.

Tubal in the Greek is written *Thubal*, and refers to a people known as Tibarenes, near the Moschian mountains. The Bible commonly joins together Tubal and Meshech, which makes it thought that they peopled countries bordering upon each other. Bochart is very copious to prove that by Meshech and Tubal are intended the Muscovites and Tiberenians.—*Calmet.*

Knobel considers the *Tibareni* to have been a branch of this widely spread Turanean family, known to the Hebrews as Tubal. This approximates to the view of Bochart (Phaleg. iii. 12) who makes the *Moschi* and *Tibareni* represent Meshech and Tubal."

Another writer says: " It is admitted that תֻּבַל *Thubl*, or *Thubal*, is the Hebrew name for the Tibareni, or Siberians, who occupied the country watered by the *Thubl*, or *Tobol*, north of the Caspian, and East of the Ural mountains. Hence, while Moscow is the capital of Meshech, Tobolski is the capital of the Thubal."

That Tubal, in connection with Rosh and Meshech, was located in what is now Russian territory is beyond question.

Persia.—Inasmuch as Persia still retains her ancient name, and her identity is indisputable, we shall waste no space in proving her whereabouts.

Ethiopia.—Called by the Hebrews Cush. It lies to the south of Egypt, and embraced, in its most extended sense, the modern Nubia, Sennaar, Kordofan, and Northern Abyssinia, and in its more definite sense, the kingdom of Maroe, from the junction of the Blue and White branches of the Nile, to the border of Egypt. The only direction in which a clear boundary can be fixed is in the North, where Syene marked the division between Ethiopia and Egypt, (Ezek. xxix. 10); in other directions the boundaries can be generally described, as the Red Sea on the East, the Libyan desert on the West, and the Abyssinian highlands on the South. It is described as a well watered country lying "by the side of" (*A. V.* "beyond") the waters of Cush (Isa. xviii. 1; Zeph. iii. 10), being traversed by the two branches of the Nile, and by the Astaboras or *Tacazze.*"—*Smith's Bible Dictionary.*

Libya.—This name is applied by Greek and Roman writers to the African continent ; generally, however, excluding Egypt. Josephus says, "it is beyond the river in the region of Mauritania. By this name it is well known in the Grecian histories; adjacent to the region which they called Phut."

Ethiopia and Libya therefore, taken together, doubtless include the whole of Northern Africa, excepting Egypt.

Gomer.—The eldest son of Japheth, and originally located in the Northern part of lesser Asia. Josephus, (Antiq. lib. i. cap. 7) tells us expressly that the Galatians, who lived in this tract, and to whom St. Paul wrote an epistle, were called Gomerites. Herodotus tells us that a people called *Cimmerii*, dwelt in these parts; and Pliny, (lib. v. cap. 3,) speaks of a town in Troas, a part of Phrygia, called *Cimmeris*; which names are plainly derived from Gomer. It is certain that Phrygia did anciently extend over a very considerable part of the northern tract of Lesser Asia. It is also certain that a great part of Galatia was formerly included under Phrygia as having been possessed by the Phrygians.

Bochart conjectures that the name Phrygia was imposed on these parts by the Greeks, in allusion to the Hebrew name, Gomer. The radix גמר

Gamar, signifies "to consume," and its derivative, *gumra*, or *gumro*, signifies a coal; whence the Greeks might be induced to bestow on it a name of like import, calling it Phrygia, the Torrid, or Burnt country, it is certain, a part of this country was specially called by the Greeks, Burnt Phrygia.

But although the original plantation of the Gomerites or *Cimmerii* was in Lesser Asia, yet Herodotus tells us that these people sent a colony to the Mæotic Lake, North of the Euxine Sea, and so gave the name of Bosphorus Cimmerius to the strait between the Euxine Sea and the Mæotic Lake, now the strait of Caffa. This colony increasing and spreading by new colonies further westward, came up the Danube, and settled in the country, which from them has been called Germany. For Diodorus Siculus, as Mr. Mede observes, affirms that the Germans had their origin from the Cimmerians; and the Jews to this day call them Ashkenazim, of Ashkenaz, as being descended from that branch of Gomer. Indeed they retain plain marks enough of their descent, both in the name Cimeri, and as they call themselves, *Germen;* which is but a small variation from Gemren or Gomren; and this last is easily contracted from Gomeren, Gomereans. For the termination *en* is a plural termination in the German language; and from the singular Gomer, is formed *Gomeren*, Gemren, by the same analogy, as from brother is formed brotheren, brethren.

The country of Gomer is in the Chaldee, named

Germia, Garmeja, but others write it Germania, Garmanaja. The later Jews by Germia understand Germany, the same as when it is written with an n, Germania, and so say the Talmudists on Gen. x. 2, "Gomer is Germanaja" (Joma, fol. x: i).— *Wells.*

It would appear from the evidence adduced, that the Germans are the descendants of Gomer, from his son Ashkenaz, and may properly be reckoned as the representatives of Gomer at the present day.

Togarmah.—Was the third and last son of Gomer, and his family were seated in the most easterly part of the nation of Gomer, north of Judea. Cappadocia was the name by which a considerable part of the lot of Togarmah was afterwards known to the Greeks. Ptolomy so locates them, as also does Strabo. It was by them also that Russian and Independent Tartary were peopled.

Sheba and Dedan.—These two are so frequently spoken of together that we thus classify them. They were both sons of Jokshan. Both were located in the districts of Arabia, and both were traders. The men of Dedan are mentioned by Ezekiel as trading in the Tyrian fairs. They carried thither the ivory and ebony which they procured from "the many isles" to the eastward, and "precious clothes for chariots." Sheba carried "the chief of spices, precious stones and gold." Their position in Arabia lay convenient to the ivory and gold, precious stones and spice countries of Africa and India. Sheba embraced the greater part of the Yemen or Arabia Felix; and Dedan the country now occupied by the Sultan of Muscat. The British power has planted itself on the soil of Sheba, occupying Aden, the Gibralter of the Red Sea and the Key of Egypt, and may properly be said to represent the Sheba of the present day. The Arabian Polyglotts by Dedan understood India.

Merchants of Tarshish, and the Young Lions thereof.—That there were two points named Tarshish is apparent —one lying to the north-west of Judea and the other south-east. Jonah embarked at Joppa, now Jaffa, a port on the Mediterranean Sea, " to flee unto Tarshish from the presence of the Lord." He must have sailed westward. But we read also that Jehoshaphat built ships at Eziongeber, a port of the Red Sea, that they might sail thence to Tarshish. It is manifest that they must sail southward towards the straits of Babelmandeb, and from thence they might steer east or north to India, or southward again along the coast of Africa. But that they crept around the Arabian coast to Hindostan is almost certain, when we remember that no compasses were in use in those days ; also the time occupied in the journey (three years) as well as the productions they were laden with on their return.

The Tarshish of the northwest produced " silver, iron, tin and lead," and traded in the fairs of Tyre. Tartessus on the southernmost coast of Spain is supposed by some to be the Tarshish that supplied these products. Spain it is known produced all these sources of wealth. And the Mediterranean Sea is called the Sea of Tarshish, and the ships sailing on her waters, the ships of Tarshish. Gibralter, being located at the point indicated—the ancient Tartessus, and being the key to the Mediterranean, may represent the Tarshish of the West. Others think that inasmuch as England was a great producer of tin, lead, iron, etc., that this was the Western Tarshish. But, in either case, England would be its modern representative, as she possesses the key to the Tarshish Sea, and occupies the Tartessus of old.

The Tarshish of the East was evidently India, as Solomon had at sea a navy of Tarshish, with the navy of Hiram, which once in three years brought "gold and silver, ivory, apes and peacocks," all of them products of India. In fact, it is affirmed, that the peacock is a native of India and nowhere else. The merchandise of both the Eastern and Western Tarshish, together with the governing power in both, identifies Britain as the Tarshish power of the present day.

But the expression "Merchants of Tarshish with all the young lions thereof," seems to settle the question so far as Great Britain is concerned, when we recollect that India has been governed for sometime by a company of merchant rulers, known as the British East India Company, a merchant sovereignty, the quarterings of whose shield are filled with young lions rampant, with the motto *"Auspicio Senatus Angliæ.* Persia was represented anciently by a Ram, and Macedonia by a Goat, and the civil and military officials under those governments were represented by young rams and young goats ; so the officials of India, or Eastern Tarshish, acting under the authority of the old Lion have adopted young lions as their symbol. "Tarshish with the young lions thereof" we may therefore reasonably conclude points to the Lion power of the Anglo-Indian Empire.

Israelites.—These need no identification, as they are found in all parts of the world, and speak the languages of all nations. Possessed, too, of vast quantities of wealth, as well as increasing influence in the centres of government and commerce, they are destined to rise to a position of greater importance than any yet experienced by them since the Lord sent them into captivity on account of their sins.

In concluding this chapter we think there need be but little if any question as to what powers and countries represent at the present time those enumerated in Ezekiel's prophecy. It has been shown that Gog is a kingly name, belonging to a royal line, as "Pharoah" belonged to the Egyptian rulers.

That Magog refers to the Scythians and Tartars, located North of the Caucasus, branching out to what is known as the Scythian country.

That Ros, Rosh, or Rhos, refers to the Russians, located on the river Araxes, or Rosh.

That Meshech was the father of the Muscovites, who occupied the country between Iberia and Armenia, and afterwards branched out to the North.

That Tubal occupied territory adjoining Meshech, and on the North his descendants were known as the Tibareni, or Asiatic Iberians, locating in the Siberian countries, in and around Tobolsk.

That all of the foregoing are located in what is now Russian territory, and are correctly represented by that great power to-day.

Gog is not only the Emperor of the land and people of Magog, but he is also "prince of Ros (Russia proper) Meshech, (Muscovy) and Tubal," (Tobolski). It is well known that Russia is an aggrandizing power, and has incorporated into her domain several kingdoms that were originally independent. In this way she has grown to enormous proportions, and is stretching out in all available directions.

It has also been shown that Persia, Ethiopia and Libya, (the Northern part of Africa,) Gomer, (Germany,) and Togarmah, (the Eastern part of Asia Minor, and Russian and Independent Tartary,) are the ones named by the prophet as allies of Gog in his great expedition against the Holy Land.

Opposed to these the names of Sheba, Dedan, and the Merchants of Tarshish are named, and it has been shown that these can be no other in our day than the British Power with her Eastern dependencies.

Having thus outlined the present representatives of the powers named in the prophecy we are now prepared to consider in greater detail the prophecy itself.

CHAPTER VII.

THE PROPHECY EXPLAINED.

At the very outset of this grand prophecy, our confidence in the exact fulfilment of every detail is inspired by the declaration that it is "the word of the Lord." Sooner may we expect the earth to stop its revolutions around the sun, or the whole vast universe to be instantly blotted out of existence, than that God's word shall fail. And what is the burden of this "word" that came unto Ezekiel?

As the representative of the Lord on earth for the time being, the Prophet is directed to set his face *against* Gog, thus declaring himself as an antagonist. That there may be no mistake as to who this Gog is, he is definitely pointed out as of the land of Magog. Not only so, but he is further identified as being "the prince of Rosh, Meshech and Tubal," which, as has been clearly shown, can refer, in our day, to no one else than he who is the prince, or chief of the Empire of Russia; an empire that now embraces within its vast domain all the countries designated. The instruction to Ezekiel, therefore, is equivalent to saying "direct thy face against the Emperor of all the Russias, and say, behold, I am against thee," etc.

The message to this mighty Emperor is not one that is full of encouragement, but, instead, is full of woe. It begins by declaring that the Lord will turn him back and put hooks into his jaws, and draw him forth with all his army and allied forces, upon the mountains of Israel.

In the thirty-ninth chapter the language is, "I will turn thee back and leave but the sixth part of thee;" or, according to the marginal reading, "I will strike thee with six plagues," or, "draw thee back with an hook of six teeth." The hook in the jaws, referred to in the thirty-eighth chapter, is here explained to be one of six teeth, and the object for which it is inserted in his jaws is to draw him forth, —"draw him, or turn him back."

The Hebrew word שׁוּב *shoov*, signifies "to turn about, to turn back, to return," hence it would seem that the Czar, at some time previous to the great invasion referred to in the prophecy, will have made a descent from his northern home, and returned again, but not to remain, for the Lord has declared that he must "turn back," or "return" from the North, but, as the sequel proves, to meet his doom. The hook of six teeth, (if we accept that rendering), is that which draws him forth, but what that hook represents, we cannot, with certainty, determine—the event alone can decide. Some have supposed that it is fulfilled, and refers to the six allied powers who turned Russia back in 1856, when she had set out with the avowed purpose of protecting the Holy Places in Jerusalem. But we think it refers rather to a turning back from the North to the South, seeing the hook, or bit in the jaw,* is for the purpose of drawing him back ; and, as the context shows, when so drawn, it is toward the land of Israel, from whence he never returns.

Or, if we accept the other marginal reading "smite thee with six plagues," then we must believe that not only will he be drawn forth, but when so drawn, and located on the mountains of Israel, he and all his multitude will be smitten with six plagues, causing their entire destruction.

There are several points which must not be lost sight of in arriving at a correct understanding of this prophecy :—

1. The time of its fulfilment is subsequent to the time when Palestine shall have been brought back from the sword, and a considerable settlement effected of Jews who are rich in gold, silver, cattle and goods.

2. That some arrangement will have been made whereby the Jews will be enabled to dwell in the land in apparent safety.

3. That the event is still future, because no such restoration has ever taken place since the dispersion, neither has any such mighty invasion, for the purpose assigned, ever taken place. Again, it was not to be until "the latter days," or "latter years;"

---

* The Hebrew word translated "hooks" refers to a kind of hook used for insertion into the noses of camels, buffaloes, bears, etc., to render them subject to be led about.

and he was to come against "the mountains of Israel which have always been waste;" therefore *subsequent* to the desolate condition in which the land has been for so many centuries past.

4. Another strong proof of its fulfilment being still future, consists in the fact that after the overthrow of the invading army, all the house of Israel are remembered by the Lord, and know Him from that day forward. The Lord gathers them to their own land, pours His spirit upon them, and turns not His face from them any more; all of which events are yet unaccomplished.

In view of these facts we may rest assured that the recent movement of Russia against Turkey is not the one contemplated in the prophecy, seeing that the Holy Land is not yet brought back from the sword, neither is it settled with a wealthy class of Israelites, nor do we find the powerful alliance existing that Ezekiel describes. But we do discover a cord of sympathy existing between Germany and Russia, and a mutual understanding with Persia, which serves to indicate what the future course of these powers will be. We also find Turkey laid powerless at the feet of her antagonist, awaiting the decision of interested powers as to her future existence. We see likewise, the Sheba, Dedan, and Tarshish power (England) appearing on the scene as the principal antagonist of Gog; and, by way of preparation for events that are clearly foreshadowed in prophecy, we see British interests gradually increasing in

Egypt, and ere long we may find that her influence in Palestine will far exceed that of any other power.

That the outcome of the recent struggle between Russia and Turkey will eventuate in the liberation of the Holy Land from the galling yoke of the Mohammedan is more than probable, and thus a way be opened up for the return of the Jews. Indeed, it may be deemed expedient to encourage the establishment of a Jewish kingdom in Palestine as a sort of barrier against Russian designs upon India. No power is so largely interested in a movement of this character as England. Therefore we may look for such a settlement of present complications as will pave the way for the fulfilment of the prophecy concerning Gog and his allies. After such an arrangement has been effected, we may expect Russia to withdraw for a season from the field, and proceed with the work of recuperation, preparatory to her last grand effort for the supremacy of the world.

Having assured ourselves that the fulfilment of the prophecy is clearly in the future, we will now return to a consideration of its details.

In describing the vast host who gather under the leadership of the Russian Czar, the prophet makes especial mention of there being many horses and horsemen, all of them clothed in all sorts of armor. It is a noteworthy fact that the Russian army is possessed of vastly more horses than any other in the world; and at the time spoken of, when they unite with their own armies the immense half civilized hordes from Northern Asia, together with those especially mentioned, from Persia, Africa, and Germany, well may it be said they are clothed in *all sorts* of armor. Such a diversity will have rarely been seen, and perhaps such a marshaling of cavalry as will then take place, the world never before witnessed.

That these armies are described as being equipped with bows, arrows, etc., proves nothing against their reference to modern nations, for the reason that the prophet describes them as they were equipped in his day, taking no note of subsequent changes, either of armaments, or names of countries and people.*

The instruction to the Czar is, "Be thou ready, and prepare thyself, thou and all thy assemblages, that are assembled about thee, and be thou a guard unto them," or "a commander over them." There has been, for a number of years past, a growing tendency towards unification, hence Germany has absorbed all her petty states, and organized a grand central government which controls the whole. So has Italy; and, indeed, there is a probability that

---

* It is a well-known fact, however, that bows and arrows, spears, swords, etc., have constituted a principal part of the armament of nations during the greater part of the period that has elapsed since the delivery of the prophecy, (nearly 2500 years ago), and that many of the tribes of Asia, who will form a large proportion of the multitude of Gog, are proficient in the use of such weapons at the present day. More civilized (?) nations, however, use breech-loading bows and arrows, and cannon-chariots, inventions of quite recent date. It is a matter of record, indeed, that as wise a man as Benjamin Franklin is reputed to have been, recommended to Congress a measure for the introduction of bows and arrows into the army of the United States as a part of its equipment.

all the smaller states of Europe and Asia will yet be swallowed up by their giant neighbors. This gathering of forces points forward to a trial of strength by the giants themselves, with a view to the mastery of the world. When the season arrives for the fulfilment of the prophecy under consideration, this centralizing process will have reached its climax. It will be allowed to go no farther, until He whose right it is to reign, shall come to claim His kingdom, and begin His righteous rule.

Ezekiel describes not only the vast realm of Persia, and all of Northern and Eastern Africa, as allied with Russia, but even Germany, with all her bands, will rally under the leadership of this mighty Autocrat of the last days. The Czar will be commander over all the vast host, and will lead them forward "into the land that is *recovering* from the sword,"—the land of Israel. The multitude of armed men seemed so great, in the eye of the prophet, that he describes them as "a cloud to cover the land;" and their impetuous movement is such as to cause him to describe it as a tempest—sudden and irresistable.

The intent of the leader is to take a great spoil—in short, to rob the returned Israelites of their wealth of gold, silver, cattle and goods.* It is possible, and

---

*It is a fact that the Jews exercise a controlling influence in the finances of the world. Their combined wealth is immense; and when a movement is inaugurated for their return to Palestine, carrying their wealth with them, we can readily see what a temptation will be presented to the avarice of the Russian Czar, to possess himself of it.

very probable, however, that he will have a further object in view, viz., the conquest of India, and that this immense host will be gathered for the purpose of a movement "*over*" the land of Israel—spoiling the Jews by the way, as he presses forward to the East. This idea is suggested from the fact that it scarcely seems probable that so formidable an army would be gathered for the mere purpose of overcoming the insignificant company of Jews who will then be gathered in Palestine. On his movements becoming known, however, an interested party meets him on the way—a party described as "Sheba, Dedan, and the Merchants of Tarshish, with all the young lions thereof," (England), who propounds to him the inquiry, "art thou come to take a spoil?" etc. His intentions are divined by this antagonist, and a disposition to thwart his purposes at the outset is manifested. But, as the sequel shows, it is not permitted to any earthly power to overthrow this giant confederacy of the last days. Its doom will be sealed from on high. Its sudden overthrow will be the beginning of a revolution in the affairs of earth.

Gog's coming had been heralded by the prophets, hence when he appears with his mighty host upon the sacred soil of Palestine, he is met with the question, "Art thou he of whom I have spoken in old time by my servants the prophets of Israel, which prophesied those days, many years, that I would bring thee against them?" Every surrounding and circumstance proves that he is, indeed, the very same—the proud Assyrian of the latter days *—the one who "shall come in like a flood," but who shall be put to flight.† For nigh 2500 years the word of the Lord concerning him has been on record, yet how few believe it. If not actually set aside as a fable, it has been grossly perverted through the spiritualizing process of interpretation. But, now that the event is near at hand, and the way is being rapidly prepared for its actual fulfilment, the folly of these semi-infidels is manifest, and their worldly wisdom is utterly confounded. The grand workings of God's providence are seen in the forward movements of His enemies, for it is His purpose now to be glorified in their very overthrow. From Heaven itself will descend the elements which shall destroy them. The Lord's fury comes up in His face; He is jealous for His people of Israel, and full of wrath against those who have come to despoil them.

It appears that the great armies will be actually present upon the mountains and plains of Judea, all unsuspecting of what awaits them. In fact, judging from what we read in Zechariah xix. 1, 2, the city of Jerusalem will be taken, and the houses rifled, and the women ravished, and half of the city carried into captivity, before the Lord interferes. He does not destroy them whilst they only *intend* to despoil Israel, but waits until the overt act is committed. Then it is that the crisis is reached. Now shall the

---

* Isaiah xxx. 27–33. † Isaiah lix. 19.

Lord go forth and fight against those nations as when he fought in the day of battle. The season of apparent non-interference in the affairs of men will have ended, and the Lord will break forth in indignation upon the assembled hosts of Gog. The time will have come for the infliction of the "six plagues" which He declared He should strike Him with, viz.: 1. Pestilence; 2. Blood; 3. A sweeping rain; 4. Vast hailstones; 5. Fire; 6. Brimstone. The Lord, when talking with Job, over 4000 years ago, referred to this day of trouble, and spoke of the implements of His warfare as being even then stored up. He asks: "Hast thou entered into the treasures of the snow? or hast thou seen the treasures of the hail which I have reserved against the day of battle and war?" *

The grand drama will apparently be inaugurated by a terrible earthquake, one that will shake not only the earth, but the sea also; yea, the mountains shall be thrown down, and every living thing on the face of the land, and even the fishes of the sea will experience the fearful convulsions of this great and mighty earthquake.

Zechariah says it shall result in cleaving in two the Mount of Olives from East to West, and half of the mountain shall be removed to the North, and the other half to the South, leaving a great valley between. He also says it shall be a day known to the Lord, "not day nor night, but it shall come to pass

---

* Job xxxviii. 22, 23.

that at evening time it shall be light." The electric disturbance of that day will be something extraordinary—a day never to be forgotten. "The light shall not be clear nor dark." The Douay version says: "And it shall come to pass in that day, that there shall be no light, but cold and frost."

The terrible "six plagues" with which the allied hosts will be stricken, will probably overtake them in the order named in the prophecy. First, "pestilence." The original word, thus translated, is דֶּבֶר *dehver*, and signifies "destruction, death; hence plague, pestilence, murrain among beasts," etc. The nature of the pestilence or plague is not specified; but Zechariah is explicit upon this point, and uses the word נֶגֶף *nahgaph*, "a stroke, blow; a spot, mark, blemish, whether eruption, scab or leprosy." And in further defining the nature of the stroke which will overtake them, he says: "This shall be the plague wherewith the Lord shall smite all the people that have fought against Jerusalem: their flesh shall consume away while they stand upon their feet, and their eyes shall consume away in their holes, and their tongue shall consume away in their mouth." A most dreadful disease, truly; its effect being to produce blindness and speechlessness among the assembled thousands of Gog. Need we wonder, then, that "it shall come to pass in that day that a great tumult from the Lord shall be among them; and they shall lay hold every one on the hand of his neighbor, and his hand shall rise up against the hand of his neighbor?"* Or, as Ezekiel predicts, that "every man's hand shall be pointed against his brother." A mutual slaughter will ensue, resulting in a fulfilment of the second plague—*blood*, or "blood-shedding," as one translator has it.

The four remaining plagues, it appears, will then be visited upon the confused and affrighted multitudes in quick succession—a sweeping rain setting in, which culminates in a dreadful shower of vast hailstones, rolling fire and brimstone. This terrible storm may be the same as that referred to in Revelation xvi. 21, where, in conjunction with an earthquake "such as was not since men were upon the earth, so mighty an earthquake and so great," there is a great hailstorm from heaven, in which every stone is about the weight of a talent (114 lbs). A similar visitation once came upon Egypt as a plague upon Pharoah. "The Lord sent thunder and hail, and the fire ran along upon the ground . . so there was hail, and fire mingled with the hail, very grievous, such as there was none like it in all the land of Egypt since it became a nation."†

Again, when the allied armies of the five Amorite kings fled from before Israel, "the Lord cast down great stones from heaven upon them unto Azekah, and they died; they were more which died with hailstones than they whom the children of Israel slew with the sword."‡

---

* Zech. xiv. 13.   † Exodus ix. 23, 24.   ‡ Joshua x. 11.

Thus we see that the plagues which will overtake Gog and his allies on the plains and mountains of Israel will not be new, but are such as have previously been inflicted. They may and no doubt will exceed in terror everything that has preceded them.

Such a scene as is depicted by the prophets Ezekiel and Zechariah no one can fully comprehend. Opening with a darkened heaven, dark even to blackness, followed by an earthquake that will exceed anything the world ever experienced, and this succeeded by a rapidly consuming plague which will eat out eyes, tongue and flesh while the men still stand upon their feet; then a wild tumult, all military order and discipline gone,—even the many horses that accompany the expedition being visited with the consuming plague, and of course rendered unmanageable, what a terrible scene must ensue under such circumstances! But as if this were not enough, the pent up treasures of rain, hail, fire and brimstone, which, like a death pall, has been hanging over them in the darkened heavens, are now poured out in dreadful fury upon their ungodly heads, the storm gathering in intensity until every man and every beast of that immense multitude are offered up as a sacrifice to the birds and wild beasts of the field, who are invited to feed upon their carcasses. Thus ends the mightiest invasion the world has ever seen. Thus also will the Lord make Himself known in all the earth, but primarily to His people Israel. "Thus will I magnify myself, and sanctify myself," says the Lord, " and I will be known in the eyes of many nations; and they shall know that I am the Lord."

What an excitement will be produced in every part of the world when the news of this terrible catastrophe is flashed over the wires! What glaring head-lines will appear in the news columns of the daily press! what various ways there will be of accounting for it; and what speculations our wise editors will indulge in as to the future political prospects of the powers specially concerned! Can we imagine that one of them will be able to give their readers the true reason for such a wholesale overthrow of one of the grandest and most powerful armies the world has ever seen? Perhaps not. But whether they can or not matters but little, for it will be brought to their comprehension shortly afterwards in a way that no one can mistake, for the dashing to pieces of Gog's multitude will be but the beginning of a new era in the government of the world. The prophet Zechariah tells us that when the great earthquake shall cleave asunder the Mount of Olives, the Lord's feet shall stand upon it once more. And after describing the effect of the earthquake, he tells us that "the Lord my God shall come, and all the saints with thee." Thus we see that the resurrection of the dead (those who fell asleep in Christ), will have taken place *previously*, and of course the change to immortality of the living, and the removal of the whole band to meet the

Lord in the air will also have passed; and when the allied forces of Gog meet with their overthrow in Israel's land, then it is that the Lord shall descend from heaven in power and great glory—then shall He come with ten thousand of His saints from heaven, and execute judgment upon His enemies. * And Zechariah adds that from thenceforth "the Lord shall be King over all the earth ; in that day shall there be one Lord and His name one."

The magnitude of the host that will be slain on the mountains of Israel may be divined when we remember that those who dwell in the cities of Israel will gather together a sufficiency of implements of war to serve them as fuel for seven years, so as to obviate all necessity of procuring wood from field or forest. And the house of Israel will be occupied for seven months in burying the mighty host in a valley selected for the purpose.

Having destroyed utterly this giant enemy of Israel, the Lord declares "now will I bring again the captivity of Jacob, and have mercy upon the *whole house* of Israel." These who had been previously gathered in the holy land were a rich and prosperous people, returned from the land that was recovering from the sword, but they did not comprise the whole house of Israel. They were a remnant who had settled in the midst (or navel) of the land; in the highest part of it; or in the neighbor-

---

* 1 Cor. xv. 51-54; 1 Thess. iv. 13-17; Jude 14, 15; Zech. xiv. 3-9.

hood of Jerusalem. But when the whole house of Israel is gathered they will occupy not only the midst of the land but will scarcely find room for their numbers in the land itself. *

---

* Isaiah xlix. 19, 20.

CHAPTER VIII.

CONCLUSION.

The long cherished hope of Israel, of returning one day to the land of their fathers, will at last be realized. Their expectation of meeting also the promised Messiah will also be fulfilled; but oh how differently from what they expected. Like the brethren of Joseph, who found in him whom they had virtually slain, a Savior from death, at a time when deliverance was shut out from every other source, they will find in Jesus, whom they slew, a Savior, when nothing but overwhelming destruction presents itself. And it may be, that, like those of old, who, on discovering their brother in such power and glory, and knowing of their previous conduct towards him, expected a visitation of wrath, so these of the latter days, on discovering that their great deliverer is none other than He with the pierced side and wounded hands, whom their fathers slew, will expect judgment instead of mercy: but as Joseph fell on the necks of his brethren and forgave all, so Jesus will graciously forgive the treatment He has received, and restore them to His favor again. "Then shall they know that I am the Lord their God which caused them to be led into captivity among the heathen; but I have gathered them into their own land, and left none of them any more there; neither will I hide my face any more from them: for I have poured out my spirit upon the house of Israel, saith the Lord God." "The Redeemer" having then " come out of Zion," will also " turn away ungodliness from Jacob." The " blindness in part which happened unto Israel until the fulness of the Gentiles be come in" will have passed away, and " so all Israel shall be saved." *

We might go on multiplying texts by the hundred upon this subject of Israel's future restoration and glory, but we forbear, believing that sufficient have been already adduced to lead those who have a disposition to do so, to investigate the word of the Lord concerning it.

With reference to the destiny of Russia, Germany, Persia and Africa, after the terrible annihilation of their combined forces in Palestine, the scriptures are explicit, that not only these kingdoms, but all others on the face of the earth, including even this proud but distracted Republic of ours, will bow submissively to the rule of Him whose law shall go forth from Zion, and whose word will go forth from Jerusalem, even He whose descent with His saints upon Mount Olivet will be accomplished at the time of Gog's overthrow. He it is that " shall judge among many people and rebuke

---

* Romans xi. 25, 26.

strong nations afar off," and, as a result, "they shall beat their swords into plowshares and their spears into pruning hooks; nation shall not lift up sword against nation, neither shall they learn war any more." *

That oft repeated prayer, "Thy kingdom come, thy will be done in earth as it is in heaven" will then be answered—the kingdom will have come, and the Lord's will be supremely executed in all the earth. "All kings shall fall down before Him; all nations shall serve Him." †

"The earthly centre of this glorious kingdom of righteousness and peace as already intimated will be Jerusalem. While all the nations of the earth will be blessed and happy, the highest position among them will be accorded to that people who have been more than all others, trodden down and oppressed; yea, who have suffered thus as the righteous judgment of God upon them for the rejection of their King and Lord. But the place of greatest dignity and glory will be given to those who, in the present interval between the sufferings of Christ and His return in glory, have shared the fellowship of His sufferings, in hope of His return. This is the church's place."

And now in conclusion, let us speak a word of warning to those of our readers, who are still unconverted. We beg of you not to be deceived,

---

* Micah iv. 2, 3. † Psalm lxxii.

nor dream of an intervening millennium before the coming of Christ to judge the earth. There will be no such thing. No one can assure you that the day of His appearing to take away His saints is at any great distance. Indeed His manifestation in glory *with* His saints cannot be said to be very far off. The day of trouble such as there never was since there was a nation even to that same time * appears to be rapidly approaching. For aught you know, your eyes may behold its terrors. Within the period of your natural life its thunders may burst upon *your* ears, and its solemnities cause *your* hearts to quake. Unless you embrace the Savior, who is still presented to you; unless your hearts are opened to believe the tidings of His mercy, and take refuge in His open arms, on you as yet alive, the terrors of the day of God may fall. Delay not to flee to Jesus, He is the ark of safety that will outride the coming storm. Oh that you might be led to seek refuge in Him. Oh that this precious covert may enclose you all!

And to you, dear brethren in Christ, let us say a parting word of warning. The character of the times we are living in is such as to require constant watchfulness on the part of each of us. Evil men and seducers wax worse and worse. Infidelity both open and covert is on the increase, and the lamp of faith burns very low. We need more than ever to

---

* Daniel xii., Matt. xxiv. 21.

frequently approach our Father in Heaven, and make known our petitions to Him, leaning upon His mighty strength in our own weakness. We must be truly separate from the surroundings and prevailing evil. Our place is to stand aloof, and to wait watchfully for the coming of our Lord. " With the struggles that are taking place around us we are not to meddle. The quarrels of earthly powers are not our quarrels. We may look on, indeed, for our God has thrown His own light upon them in His word. But while we look thereon with deep sorrow, it is not our place to interfere. Our work is happier work. We have to manifest, in deed and word, the truth, the love, the grace of Him for whom we look and long and wait. Our weapons are not carnal. The potsherds of the earth may strive with the potsherds of the earth. They may plot and counter-plot; they may scheme and counter-scheme; but *we know how it will all end.* We have been told before.

The crisis hastens. The revolutions will be sudden and momentous. We know not what a day or an hour may bring forth. Where to place the translation of the church to meet her Lord, we know not. It may be the very first stage of the crisis. Perhaps it will be so. Are we ready for it? The Lord grant that it may be so with each one of us!" Amen.

APPENDIX.

The following article appeared as an editorial in *The Israelite*, a Jewish paper, published at Cincinnati, O. in May, 1877. The editor unfortunately has adopted what are known as the Reform Views of Israel, which, in brief, amount to an abandonment of the hope so long held, of the coming of a personal Messiah, to redeem this ancient people, and instead it is expected that all the good things promised are to be realized through the natural progression of the age. This will account for the fears expressed by the editor (Dr. Wise) concerning the advance of a blighting power like Russia, when the prosperity of Israel "depends on the progress of liberty and justice."

We have reason to believe that the time is not far distant, when the veil that is over the Doctor's eyes will be suddenly removed, and he, with all others of the nation of Israel, will behold Him who was promised—the Messiah; but before that time, they will meet with some bitter disappointments and pass through deep waters of affliction. Let us not forget to pray for the peace of Jerusalem.

GOG UMAGOG.

The political regeneration of Western and Central Europe, between 1790 and 1875, has overcome the absolutism of State and Church to the extent of having limited the royal and imperial powers by constitutions, laws and parliaments, popular elections and public opinion, centering and assuming shape and form in the popular press; and having deprived the Church of her temporal power and political importance. There is left enough of feudal privileges, royal and imperial prerogatives, ecclesiastical powers, and official supremacy for another century to overcome, before there will be a state of tolerable justice for the common man, and the military despotism will be superceded by a government of law. Still a vast amount of work has been done in that direction, and there is a fair prospect that those nations will not come to rest until the rights of man shall be completely restored and secured.

One must be blind, however, and very much so, if he sees not that all these revolutions and reforms have not changed the Russian government. There is yet the same unrestrained absolutism on the throne as it was a century ago, and the man on the throne is also the pope of all the millions of Greek Catholic professors of Europe and Asia, with a power which the Pope of Rome never possessed. One pope has been dethroned, another is rising and exerting his supposed rights over his subjects in Turkey. Protestants and Catholics hate each other intensely ; therefore they watch each other jealously, and are always ready to curtail each other's power. Between the two a new political state of affairs could grow up and supersede them both. There is no Protestant element, no opposition of much weight in Russia against the Emperor-Pope's absolutism with his autocratic and theocratic powers to which one hundred millions of people are subjected directly or indirectly. Outside of the Russian Empire, the Greek Catholics of Austria, small in number anyhow, are given up as stray sheep. But there is one opposition to Russia's absolute power over those hundred millions of people, and the further progress of it, and that is the Islam with its Sultan. Hitherto this has been the insurmountable barrier to the Pope at St. Petersburgh. You drive out the Turks of Europe, and the situation is suddenly changed. You have a pope at St. Petersburg who is in possession of absolute power over one hundred millions of people, one-half of which belong to half-civilized nationalities, like the shepherds of Bosnia and Herzegovina, the hunters and fishermen of Montenegria, the Cossacks on the Don River, the trappers in the Ural Mountains, and the frosted hordes of Siberia. Here you have a state of the Middle Ages reproduced in 1877 as completely as could possibly be made. Next the crusades come. Let Russia overthrow the Islam in Europe, and the crusades are before the door of Central and Western Europe.

APPENDIX. 117

מִצָּפוֹן תִּפָּתַח הָרָעָה. "From the North cometh the evil over all the inhabitants of the earth," said the prophet Jeremiah, and this appears to be verified once more. Civilized Europe has but one enemy to fear, and that is Russia, which might stop it in its onward march. It has the power and the will to do it. It is the *Gog Umagog* of the Jewish legend, of whom it is said that the Messiah could not reign until *Gog Umagog* shall be slain upon the mountains of Israel. The Islam is no better and no worse than the Greek Catholic Church, but they are each other's efficient opposition, and so they are beneficial to humanity. The Turk has yielded and proclaimed a constitution on the basis of equality, and Russia is yet the fortress of uncompromising absolutism.

Russia is traditionally מַלְכוּת יָוָן *Malchuth Yavan* or *Ivan*, which has never benefited any race, never shown mercy to any people. Turkey is traditional מַלְכֵי יִשְׁמָעֵאל מַלְכֵי חֶסֶד הֵם. Ishmael, and "the kings of Ishmael are gracious kings," who have benefited many, and shown mercy to the oppressed in a thousand instances. Take away the Turk from the Russian frontiers, and Europe is in danger to be overpowered by barbarian hordes from the Northern forests, fighting for the Greek cross against the Roman cross and Protestant heretics as wildly and fanatically as the crusaders did for the supposed holy sepulchre.

If American politicians and statesmen can not see this, it is, perhaps, because they are ignorant of Russia. They travel, go through Moscow, St. Petersburg, and a few more cities, converse with aristocrats, and leave the country as ignorant as they entered it. They know the last will of Peter the Great, but know not that it is to-day the key-note of Russian policy as it was then. They judge Russia by America, but in America the policy changes, because its government is the popular one ; in Russia the same family with the same prejudices, traditions and interests since Peter the Great is still in power, and pursues the same policy precisely. American politicians and statesmen are excusable if they are ignorant of Russia, as our ambassadors to foreign courts are mostly ignorant of the language and history of the country to which they go, and are recalled before they can learn much besides the aristocratic tone and manners. In Europe this state of affairs must be well known to thousands of unprejudiced thinkers; but many of the statesmen in power are too wicked or too impotent to impress it on the minds. Some of them like to see a strong barrier set up to the progressive tendencies of Central and Western Europe steering rapidly into universal democracy, against which a powerful Russia is the best antidote; and among those "some" there are the emperors, kings, princes, and the whole host of high-born men and women, whose echoes and slaves reach into all strata of society. Some are poisoned and blindfolded by religious prejudices against the Islam, and among them the ecclesiastical dignitaries, especially in Protestant countries. Again, others like to see a war anyhow and anywhere. They have been drilled as soldiers with false conceptions of honor and right, and delight in a fight, as do our rowdies. If Russia wins, they will worship Russia; if the Turk wins, they will worship him no less. With them the fight is the object of man's existence, and the success in a fight is the highest demonstration of humanity and divinity. These plagues of society abound everywhere, only that in the aristocratic circles they wear sabres and spurs. Again, others like to see a war somewhere to make money out of it, as the picaroons of stranding ships. This sort of civilized waylayers abound in all parts of the world. Take together all these classes, the rulers, the soldiers, the high nobility and the money bags, and you find it quite natural that Europe is betrayed on this occasion again.

This war, in our estimation, is the beginning of a new era of reaction in the political affairs of Europe. However it will end, it will enlarge the Russian power, and thus strengthen the barriers set up against progress which many European statesmen wish to see. Every retrogression terrifies us in behalf of humanity, and in behalf of Israel, whose prosperity depends on the progress of liberty and justice, and is threatened by every retrogression.

www.ingramcontent.com/pod-product-compliance
Lightning Source LLC
Chambersburg PA
CBHW020126170426
43199CB00009B/659